Frontend Engineering II: Pro CSS

The Frontend Engineering Series

Frontend Engineering II: Pro CSS

CSS 1
CSS 2.1
CSS 3

Martin Rinehart

Frontend Engineering II: Pro CSS

Copyright 2014

Knowit Publishing, LLC

Hudson Valley, New York, USA

Designed and Written in LibreOffice Writer, Published to PDF, all in the USA.

Printed as near to our customers as our technology permits.

Table of Contents

Introduction

CSS is a "declarative" language with which you add styles to your HTML. Declarative computer languages let you describe what you want done without the step-by-step, how-to-do-it instructions that computers need to actually do something. "I'd like a solid blue border, five pixels wide, around this paragraph," is a declarative statement. In CSS that's

```
border: solid blue 5px;
```

The original dream behind CSS was to help the World-Wide Web graduate from a system for sharing academic papers to a system capable of displaying pages just as attractive as magazine pages. CSS brings that goal within reach. And far more.

While you learn to style your pages with CSS you'll work on upgrading the HTML-only site you built in *Volume I: Pro HTML* to a stylish, 21st century site.

Before we're done we'll explore some CSS 3, learning how to add two types of animation to our pages. This is far beyond the early dreams of "magazine-quality" presentation, approaching the field of "television-quality" presentation. In fact, it goes beyond television, because the viewer is an active, not passive, participant.

Along the way, we'll leave the 20th century's single focus on desktop computers. Instead we'll enter the 21st century world of smartphones, tablets and monitors of all sizes. Your website project will look good on every device bigger than a wristwatch and smaller than a 4K monitor.

Enjoy the journey!

1 Write Your First CSS

This is a "knowit" (knowledge unit). That means (in this case) that it has an online part, as well as this print part. The online part is at:

MartinRinehart.com

We'll point to locations in the online work with a "drilldown":

```
Online: Knowits > CSS II > Welcome
```

You click "Knowits" on the first menu at MartinRinehart.com. The second line of menus appears (if it was not already there). You click "CSS II," and click "Welcome" on the third menu. The "Welcome" screen explains the knowit. Skip it if you are a veteran of *Pro HTML*.

If you are not a veteran of *Pro Html*, this knowit continues right now at

```
Online: Knowits > CSS II > Welcome
```

Warning: If you want to learn to write CSS you must follow the drilldowns to the online portions. They include specific code information and coding assignments. Just reading this text is no more likely to succeed than just reading *How to Ride a Bicycle*. To learn to ride a bicycle, you have to sit on the seat and pedal. To write CSS, you have to get your fingers on your keyboard and write CSS.

Knowit Recap

A knowit, knowledge unit, can combine media. This one combines print and online. Print is easier to read. (There are about a quarter million "pixels" in a square centimeter of this print. There are about 800 pixels in a square centimeter of a typical desktop monitor.) But putting your mouse on the printed page and clicking is not going to get you anywhere. Both media have advantages, so we use both.

Now, off to the Companion page, the start of the knowit for this chapter:

Online: Knowits > CSS II > Online > 1

(We hope you noticed that if "Knowits" and "CSS II" were already punched, it took just two clicks to get to "Online" and then "1". A great goal of all frontend engineering: make the visitors job simple!)

Now, let's get started. Go Online 1a will help you create a template if you don't have one already.

Online: Knowits > CSS II > Online > 1 > 1a

Then we'll begin with a few words about the history of CSS before we dive into styling with Cascading Style Sheets.

History

HTML was barely out of diapers when people discovered the need for style sheets. (To be more exact, they discovered that repeatedly adding the same attributes to every heading in a document, for example, was tedious work. The kind of work for which computers were better suited than were people.)

Håkon Wium Lie, of Opera, and Bert Bos (author of an early browser), who would later join the W3C and chair the CSS working group, implemented an experimental style sheet language to show what could be done. This language was proposed as an adjunct to HTML as early as 1994, just five years after Tim Berners-Lee invented the World-Wide Web and HTML.

This started what was to become CSS on the very bumpy road that would lead it, today, to being a comfortable standard from which we all benefit.

Cascading Style Sheets

CSS is an abbreviation for "cascading style sheets." It occasionally refers to style sheets in a cascade. More often it refers to the styles that can be specified on such sheets. They can be specified in, among other places, your "markup."

The "markup" refers to your HTML files which, if you started with a finished written document, not for the web, and then added tags, could be said to have been "marked up."

What Are Styles?

The basic idea of CSS is that you start with content in your HTML (semantics) and then use style rules to specify the finished look of the document (presentation). Style rules specify fonts (sizes, weights, families), colors, layout and more. Style rules are also available for aural and other non-visual documents, though these are beyond the scope of this knowit.

Rules

Note: When you refer to CSS "rules," as we do here, you exclude CSS's "at-rules" (they start with an "@" character). We introduce at-rules in Chapter 6.

A CSS rule has two parts:

- A "selector" choosing the element(s) to which it applies.
- A "declaration" that specifies the styling to apply.

```
selector { declaration }
```

The declaration is wrapped in braces (not parentheses) as shown.

```
         Braces: { } Parentheses: ()
```

The declaration also has two parts:

- A "property" name.
- The property's value.

The following rule would provide a light brown background for all your <h2> headings:

```
h2 { background-color: wheat }
```

Values are often the same as the values you use for HTML attributes. The color wheat is also the color #f5deb3. Unlike HTML attribute values, you do not use quotes around the values in CSS except when a single value includes space characters:

```
font-family: 'Times New Roman'
```

Places for Rules

CSS rules go in the style attribute of any HTML tag, or in separate style sheets. (The style attribute is universal in HTML 4.01, global in HTML 5.)

Styling a Single HTML Element

This is a style applied to a single heading:

```
<h2 style='background-color: wheat'>
    Whole Wheat for Healthy Eating
</h2>
```

The `style` attribute's value is enclosed in quotes (it is an HTML attribute value and includes a space). The `wheat` value of the CSS property `background-color` is not quoted.

Try inline styles on your own. Go Online 1b explains how:

Online: Knowits > CSS II > Online > 1 > 1b

An Embedded Style Sheet

Styling a document one element at a time gets tiresome very quickly (as was discovered in the early days of HTML). Also, if you style every heading differently, your site's visitors would get tired, very quickly. The easy way, and the best, is to create a style sheet that specifies how elements are styled. Embedded style sheets (there may be more than one) go in your HTML's <head> section, as Listing 1-1 shows.

Listing 1-1

```
<head>
    <style>
        h1 { background-color: wheat}
        h2 { background-color: wheat}
        h3 { background-color: wheat}
    </style>
</head>
<body>...
```

As with HTML, the use of whitespace, such as the indenting shown in Listing 1-1, is entirely optional. Our format has evolved to make our style sheets easy to read and easy to modify. To try it yourself, add an embedded style sheet into your own page, and style all the paragraph elements as Go Online 1c shows.

Online: Knowits > CSS II > Online > 1 > 1c

External Style Sheets

Style sheets may also be placed in their own files. If your website has multiple pages, this is the technique that lets you provide a single style sheet that every page will use. You incorporate the style sheet with a `<link>` tag in the `<head>` section. We'll show the details later in this chapter.

Grouping Rules

To make your job simpler (and to encourage good styling) you may group multiple selectors in front of a single declaration, this way:

```
h1, h2, h3 { background-color: wheat }
```

And you may use multiple declarations in a single declaration block, separating them with semicolons, as in Listing 1-2:

Listing 1-2

```
h1, h2, h3 {
    background-color: wheat;
    color: SaddleBrown;
}
```

(`SaddleBrown` is a dark brown. The `color` property is the color of the text.)

An extra semicolon following the last declaration is permitted and we always use it (which means we never forget to add the necessary semicolon when we add another declaration in a declaration block).

Selectors

We've shown HTML tags as selectors. In CSS these are called "type selectors." This is only one of a wide range of possibilities. We'll present four more here; that will be enough for this chapter's work.

Class Selectors

Another HTML attribute that is universal (and global) is the `class`. If you want some elements of your page to be a bit larger than most you could create an `oversize` class. If you want some elements to use blue type (the default is black) you could create a `blue_text` class. Your markup could look like Listing 1-3.

Listing 1-3

```
<p>Plain paragraph.</p>
<p class='oversize'>
      Larger type here.</p>
<p class='blue_text'>
      Blue type here.</p>
<p class='oversize blue_text'>
      Larger, blue text!</p>
```

Without CSS (or JavaScript) a class designation is meaningless. With CSS you can make classes real. You precede the class name with a period in your style sheets, as Listing 1-4 shows.

Listing 1-4

```
<style>
      .blue_text { color: blue; }
      .oversize { font-size: 1.2em; }
</style>
```

(Not familiar with the `em` size? From old typography, an em was the width of the letter "M" in the font in use. In CSS it specifies size relative to the current font. `1.2em` is twenty percent larger than the current size.)

Try Go Online 1d for using classes:

Online: Knowits > CSS II > Online > 1 > 1d

ID Selectors

Another universal/global HTML attribute is the ID. That is a unique identifier (you are responsible for ensuring that it is unique) you assign to a single element. We use ID selectors constantly and the result is much more readable than doing the same job with inline styles.

To use an ID in the style sheet, you precede it with a number sign: "#". This is commonly called a "hash" and sometimes "pound sign." We prefer "hash" as our British cousins might think of a different symbol (£) when one says "pound sign."

Listing 1-5 shows two elements styled in an embedded style sheet.

Listing 1-5

```
<head>
    <style>
        #foo {
            /* styles for 'foo' here */
        }
        #bar {
            /* styles for 'bar' here */
        }
    </style>
</head>
<body>

<p id='foo'>Foo styles for me.</p>

<p id='bar'>Bar styles here.</p>
```

In Go Online 1e we style a link (which will be needed in the next section.)

Online: Knowits > CSS II > Online > 1 > 1e

Pseudo-Class Selectors

Now we get to another selector alternative used regularly in places such as navigation menus: the pseudo-class :hover. Unlike other classes, it is chosen by user action. When the user moves the mouse pointer over an element, the element joins the :hover pseudo-class (until the mouse pointer leaves).

A common way to style links to other pages in a navigation menu is to change the cursor from the default arrow to the pointing finger. These are values default and pointer of the cursor property. You might want to change the links' background color from its default (possibly the page background) to white, to emphasize the fact that the mouse is over an active element. Listing 1-6 shows a common treatment for navigation links.

Listing1-6

```
<style>
    .nav {
        cursor: default;
        /* other styles here */
    }
    .nav:hover {
        background-color: white;
        cursor: pointer;
    }
```

The viewer's browser will change style from nav to nav:hover automatically as the mouse pointer moves over and away from elements in the nav class. (Warning: this is great for desktops and laptops, but smaller devices use finger gestures, not mice.)

Descendant Selectors

This is a selector with a fancy name, but a simple meaning. If one element is enclosed in another, it is called a "child" element. If a child element has its own children, the child, its children, the children's children and so on, are all called "descendants" of the first element. (You may still see the older, CSS 2 term, "contextual selector" used for descendant selectors.) In our project site, we have the menu built as Listing 1-7 shows.

Listing 1-7

```
<div id="nav" align='left'>
    <font ...> Home </font> ...
    <a ...> Timeline </a> ...
    <a ...> Map </a> </a> ...
    <a ...> Galileo </a> ...
    . . .
</div> <!-- nav →
```

Note that the `<a>` elements are all descendants of a `<div>` element. A CSS selector to choose such elements is:

```
div a { /* declarations here */ }
```

Warning, `div a` (separated by a space) selects the a elements that are descendants of a `div` element. `div, a` (with a comma) selects all `div` and all a elements. Watch for those commas!

Some CSS declarations have shortcuts. You could set border properties, as Listing 1-8 shows:

Listing 1-8

```
selector {
    border-color: blue;
    border-style: solid;
    border-width: 3px;
}
```

You can also save some typing and get the same result the `border` shortcut, this way:

```
selector { border: blue solid 3px; }
```

(The property values in a shortcut may be in any order. solid is a border style. It is not a color or length.)

This is one of those things that is more trouble to explain than it is to do. We like things that are easy to do. Giving all the links inside the nav div an outset border can be done with this line:

```
#nav a { border: blue outset 2px; }
```

That selects all the a elements that are descendants of the element whose ID is nav and sets their borders. You'll put this into practice in your project, which comes next.

Project

Are you a veteran of *Pro HTML*, the first volume in this series? If you are, the project work here adds styles to your sample project. If you are not, you will have to create (or use an existing) sample, HTML-only project Either way, be sure you save your project before you begin adding styles. You will want to go back later to compare the styled to the unstyled version.

If you have a project from *Pro HTML,* proceed immediately to Go Online 1f:

```
Online: Knowits > CSS II > Online > 1 > 1f
```

If you came here from another background, you'll need to create a sample project. This is not as hard as it might sound. Visit our sample, here:

```
Online: Knowits > CSS II > Project
```

You'll need a similar information-only website for the project examples here. For starters, create a home page with links to a few subordinate pages. Let's assume you are a fan of Jane Austen's novels. Start with a Jane Austen page and then create a page for each of her novels. The novel pages can be as simple as an `<h1>` heading with the novel title, and either your cogent essay re Fanny Price as the heroine of *Mansfield Park* or, if you are pressed for time, some *lorem ipsum*.

The important part, for our purpose, is that each page have a menu of links to the other pages at the top. See the project in the HTML volume for what yours should look like:

Online: Knowits > HTML I > Project

As we go along, add features to your project to roughly match our sample, before styles (HTML only) and then style them.

With your sample project, and it's very simple navigation links, you are ready to go on to add an external style sheet, as shown in Go Online 1f.

Online: Knowits > CSS II > Online > 1 > 1f

Quiz

Choose the word or phrase that best completes each sentence.

1) CSS stands for
   a) Corinthian Styling System.
   b) Cascading Style System.
   c) Cascading Style Sheets.

2) CSS was invented
   a) when the World-Wide Web was five years old.
   b) when the Internet bubble burst.
   c) when Google created the Chrome browser.
   d) to create HTML element attributes.

3) CSS rules have
   a) two parts, a property name and a value.
   b) two parts, a custom and a valuation.
   c) a head and a body.
   d) none of the above.

4) CSS rules may be placed
   a) inline, out-of-line or in style sheets.
   b) inline or in embedded or external style sheets.
   c) in cascading or flat-water styles.

5) Style sheets may group
   a) selectors.
   b) declarations.
   c) both of the above.

6) Class selectors
   a) may be separated by commas.
   b) segregate HTML tags by the tags' "value."
   c) apply only to HTML 4 and 4.01.
   d) are used to identify specific HTML elements.

7) ID selectors
   a) are preceded with dollar signs in the style sheet.
   b) are preceded with pound signs in the style sheet.
   c) are preceded with hash marks in the style sheet.

8) Pseudo-class selectors
   a) may always be determined in advance.
   b) may only be determined during operation.
   c) may be determined by the mouse position.

9) Descendant selectors
   a) eliminate the elements that "inherit" from a parent.
   b) apply to elements that are not direct child elements.
   c) do not include sibling elements.
   d) include sibling elements.

10) HTML tag selectors
   a) cannot be descendant selectors.
   b) must have matching ID values.
   c) may be part of descendant selectors.
   d) must follow class selectors.

2 The Box Model

Since CSS 1, our style sheets have been built on boxes. Every tag that creates something you see on your screens creates a box. Every box may be styled with CSS, whether it be a paragraph of text, an image or a heading. When you added padding and borders in Chapter 1 you were working with the CSS box model. We'll take a quick look at how this came about, and then dive in.

We'll present dozens of new properties, but you'll find them so nicely organized, so regular, that your memory will not be challenged.

History

By 1994, Lie and Bos had a browser with support for their CHSS (Cascading HTML Style Sheets) language. The "H" would be dropped when it was seen that there was no reason to limit the language to just supporting HTML. (One fears this was a triumph of ambition over focus.)

The W3C (headed by Berners-Lee) decided that, in general, this was a good idea and formally charged the HTML working group with working on the project. Lie and Bos were the technical leaders, so it is no surprise that CSS emerged (and not competing specifications, such as Netscape's JSSS—JavaScript Style Sheets).

Moving quickly, as the proposal did not have the disadvantage of numerous implementations and users, the first CSS standard, CSS 1, was completed in late 1996.

When is a standard not a standard? When it is not followed. Browser vendors were slow to adopt CSS. Those that did adopt it did so only partially. The poor frontend engineer who wanted to use style sheets could not count on pages looking the same in any two browsers (either different vendor's browsers, or different versions of a single vendor's browser).

It would be years before style sheets were a practical reality in the frontend engineers' world, but CSS 1 is still very much with us today. Its properties for styling fonts, for example, are the ones that we use every day. Among its best achievements is the definition of the CSS box model, which is this chapter's subject.

Box Areas

Almost every HTML tag creates a box. The few that don't are excluded for sensible reasons. Our `<link>` and `<style>` tags in the `<head>` are examples of elements without boxes—the viewer cannot see them. In the `<body>`, the `<br>` tag does not have a box. (The text into which it inserts a break has boxes. You can see the text.)

Boxes have three or four areas (clarification coming shortly) that you work with regularly. Figure 2-1 shows the basic idea.

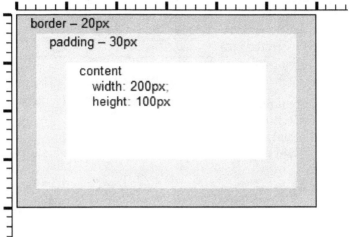

border – 20px
padding – 30px
content
width: 200px;
height: 100px

Figure 2-1

Content

The content area is the container for text, images, headings or whatever you need. Note that content may or may not fit. Commonly, scroll bars will appear as needed. Note that Figure 2-1 shows 200×100 pixels of content. This is the CSS size of the box, though the outside of its borders measure 300×200 pixels.

Padding

Boxes, especially boxes with borders, need a bit of padding around their content. Figure 2-2 shows text without padding and with padding.

Figure 2-2

The second box has three pixels of padding all around. You see a dramatic difference between the left-hand sides of the two boxes.

Lorem ipsum dolor sit amet, consectetuer adipiscing elit, sed diam nonummy nibh euismod tincidunt ut laoreet dolore magna aliquam erat volutpat.

Note that the first box is 250 pixels wide. To make them look the same, the

Duis autem vel eum iriure dolor in hendrerit in vulputate velit esse molestie consequat, vel illum dolore eu feugiat nulla facilisis at vero eros.

second box is 244 pixels wide (plus three pixels padding, left and right).

Border

The boxes in Figure 2-2 have `border-style: double` borders. You've already seen the `border-width` and `border-color` properties in use, as well as the `border` shorthand property. The boxes in Figure 2-2 are `border: black double 3px`.

This is a good time to look at all the values of the `border-style` property, in code, shown in Go Online 2a:

Online: Knowits > CSS II > Online > 2 > 2a

Be aware that browsers, especially MSIE, take liberties with your colors as they darken/lighten to show the effect of shadows. As with HTML, view the results in all the browsers you want to support.

Margin

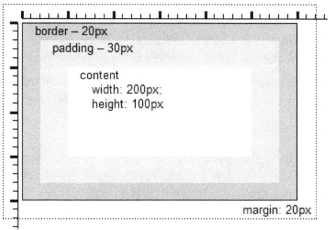

Figure 2-2

Figure 2-2 illustrates the margin that is the fourth of our "three or four" box areas. You may consider margins a box area, or you may claim they are clearly outside the box. We will agree with you either way. Margins cover nothing, letting the background show. You use them to provide spacing between your elements.

Horizontal Margins

Horizontal margins do not collapse. If the right side of one box has a 20-pixel margin, and the left-side of an adjacent box has a 10-pixel margin you get 30 pixels between the boxes.

Vertical Margins

Vertical margins are collapsed. A 20-pixel margin above or below a 10-pixel margin will combine, leaving only a 20-pixel margin.

Properties for Four Sides

So far we have used declarations like `padding: 3px`. This is the common usage, specifying padding on all four sides. We could also specify padding on the left side with `padding-left`. You can use `-top`, `-right` and `-bottom` to specify the other sides.

This should be good news if you were wondering how to remember so many style properties. You knew one, `padding`, and now you know five: `padding`, `padding-left`, `padding-top`, `padding-right` and `padding-bottom`.

Similarly, there are five possibilities for `margin`. Better yet, you have `borderX` (where X is `-top`, `-right`, `-bottom`, `-left` or omitted) and `borderXY` (where Y is one of `-color`, `-style`, `-width` or omitted). That gives you 20 different properties for just the `border`.

You can also specify one or four values for these properties: `border-color: red;` or `border-color: red blue cyan yellow;`. One color applies to all borders. Four colors applies clockwise starting from the top.

Specifying two or three colors also has defined meanings which we will not explain. (You can google if you are curious.) We tell you this as you may sometimes see other CSS experts showing off by applying this knowledge. Please don't become one of them. Specifying each border by name, when you want different borders on different sides, is a much better practice.

You might want to view our cautionary page re mixing different widths in a single border: http://martinrinehart.com/frontend-engineering/artists/other/border-radius-limits.html

Stick to a single border width, all around.

Position

In this chapter we will introduce the positioning of your boxes, as if it were a simple matter. Sometimes this is all you need to know. In Chapter 3 we go into positioning in more detail, as it is not, in reality, a simple matter.

Containers

First, everything is positioned relative to something else. Most commonly, boxes are positioned in containing boxes. At the outermost level, your HTML has a root element, `<html>`, that probably contains `<head>` and `<body>` elements. The `<body>` contains the visible elements. You may create `<div>`s that contain text and images. The text and images are positioned within their `<div>`s. The `<div>`s are positioned within the `<body>` (or within other elements, commonly other `<div>`s).

X, Y Positioning

The X and Y axes of the screen are not those you remember from math classes. X is horizontal, increasing from zero on the left. Y is vertical, increasing downward from zero at the top.

The main way to position elements is by setting their `left` (x) and `top` (y) properties. These are commonly set in pixels or percentages. Percentages are fractions of the container's size. It may be convenient to set `right` (x) and `bottom` (y) properties. Remember that results are not guaranteed if you provide styles for both (`left` and `right`, or both `top` and `bottom`).

The next examples illustrate the main ideas of x and y positioning. Begin by trying to answer this question: Where is `top:0px; left:0px` going to put one box, contained in another? (Assume they both have `borders` and `padding`.) We suggest you try Go Online 2b.

Online: Knowits > CSS II > Online > 2 > 2b

Next, suppose you wanted a contained box to live in the corner of a container box. Assume that you mean to place the contained box's border exactly over the container's border in one corner, as Figure 2-3 shows.

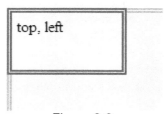

Figure 2-3

You want to understand the box model so completely that you can get this correct in every corner. Here are two hints. First, the position values (`left`, `top`, etc.) may be negative,. Second, `right: nnpx` means "inside the right of the container by nn pixels" (the mirror image of `left`). Go Online 2c makes this clear.

Online: Knowits > CSS II > Online > 2 > 2c

Z-Index Positioning

If you use just HTML it is the browser's job to ensure that items are laid out so they do not overlap. If you use CSS, it is easy to create overlapping boxes. When boxes overlap, which one should be on top (closer to the viewer, hiding items behind it)?

The simple rule is items are painted in the order they appear in the markup. If you don't want this order, you have two alternatives. One is to use the `z-index` property. The `z-index` is a number, an integer that you assign. It defaults to zero. You may use negative numbers. Boxes are drawn on the screen in `z-index` order.

To be more exact, boxes in the same "stacking context" are drawn in `z-index` order or, if z indices are the same, in the order they appeared in the markup. Each container element establishes its own stacking context. An element with `z-index:10` may be hidden behind an element with `z-index:3` if they are not in the same stacking context.

If you are beginning to think this is not simple, we refer you to the actual CSS 2.1 specification (subsection 9.9.1, linked on the Companion Page) for the full rules. They are frightfully complex. We said there were two alternatives.

The second alternative is to simply rearrange elements in the markup. Elements that you want in front of others should be specified after all the elements they might overlap. If your markup is in back-to-front order, the `z-index` need never be specified. This almost always works. Use comments in the markup as necessary to explain otherwise strange orders.

See Chapter 3 for some of the many exceptions to common ordering on the z axis.

Size

In HTML, block-level elements (`<div>`, `<p>`, `<h?>`, etc.) are as wide as the container and as tall as the content requires. Inline elements are as wide as need be, wrapping to successive lines as required. CSS lets you get in the way.

If you specify height for a block-level element, the content may not fit. (An issue on the desktop, a major concern on tablets and phones.) If you specify width and height, inline elements may not fit. CSS lets you specify the layout, and gives you the power to cause problems.

Width and Height

You can specify the width and/or height with the `width` and `height`
properties. See the discussion below, "Position and Size Values," for the
units you can use.

Minimums and Maximums

In addition to specifying a normal width with the `width` property, you
can specify a `min-width` and/or a `max-width`. These will be critical
for pages that may be viewed on anything from a phone to a desktop
monitor. Go Online 2d shows you how to simulate different devices by
dragging your browser's side in and out.

> Online: Knowits > CSS II > Online > 2 > 2d

Position and Size Values

Percentages

If you set sizes in percentages (e. g., `width: 50%`) your sizes will be
relative to your container element. The ultimate container for everything
that you see is `<body>`, which will be, at least initially, sized based on
the device size of the viewing hardware (phone, tablet, laptop, etc.).

Pixels

Pixels, a contraction of "picture elements" are the actual dots on the
screen, until you start building with HTML and CSS. Paint a div, in your
mind's eye, 100 pixels square. (There are 72 pixels per inch, just under
30 per cm, on many monitors.) The pixel density of many phones and
tablets is higher; a true 100-pixel square's size will depend on the device
pixel density.

But assume you are looking at a 100 pixel square on a 72 pixels-per-inch monitor. Now zoom in 20%. What happens? The physical pixels don't change. Your "logical" pixels are now each 1.2 physical pixels in size. Your browser is working hard to map logical pixels, specified in CSS, into physical pixels. Remember that you have lots of viewers and every one of them can zoom in or out, to suit their devices and eye sights. So how big is a pixel?

The simple answer is, you don't know. You can't know unless you know about the zoom level and the hardware.

We use pixel lengths all the time, in the simple expectation that our viewers have already set their hardware/browser combinations to be comfortable with the average pixels they view in cyberspace. That these may or may not be physical pixels doesn't worry us. 100 pixels on a desktop is longer than 100 pixels on a phone, but this is often just right as phones are usually viewed closer to the eye than desktop monitors.

A hundred pixels is specified `100px`.

Standard Length Measures

If we don't know how big a pixel is, we certainly don't know how long an inch or a centimeter is. We never use standard (non-cyberspace) lengths, but they are `in`, `cm` and `mm` if you want to try them. In theory these are the precisely specified lengths. In practice, your viewers' zoom settings change them. (You cannot zoom a physical ruler, thank goodness.)

Typographic Units

There are four old-fashioned typographic units available. The `em` and the `ex` were, in the printer's world, the width of an "M" and the height of an "x" in the font in use. The point, `pt`, and the pica, `pc`, are old English print units, 1/72nd of an inch per point, 12 points per pica. The type size in this book is 11 points. (11 and 11.5 are common sizes for books.)

Since a point is 1/72nd of an inch and a monitor may show 72 pixels per inch, a point is equal to a pixel, right? Well, that convenient identity disappears with different device pixel densities, zoom levels and so on. We set font sizes in points and ems.

An em (in CSS, em) is a very useful size. It has been redefined to mean "relative to the current font size." You can use it with decimal values, so 1.2em is 20% larger than the current base font size. If you set font-size:12pt (a good size for desktop use, generally too large for phones) 1.2em is 14.4pt. 14pt is a useful <h3> heading size.

One convention suggests that you set the font-size of the <body> in pt and then set all other font sizes in em. That way changing the body font size changes all type sizes on your page. If your entire site uses a single CSS file, one change will do for every page in your site.

Another school (see the link to Bert Bos's paper on the Companion page) suggests that you don't set the body font size and then use ems to set all other sizes relative to the body font. The body font will be the browser default, as adjusted by the user (presumably) to match hardware capabilities and eyesight.

Yet another opinion holds that so many sites use 12 point type your viewer's browser is adjusted to suit that size. If you don't specify 12 points for the <body> you are defeating, not cooperating with, your viewers preferences.

As time goes on we've become more partial to the "12 points for the body and everything else in ems" approach. Whichever you choose, it will be wrong for some of your viewers, so pick one and stick to it.

You now know enough about the box model and positioning boxes to do very useful work, as you will in the project assignment. In the next chapter, we'll go into some of the less obvious details.

Project

In the bottom-left corner of our HTML project we added an extra set of navigation links, as an outline. Part of it is shown in Figure 2-4.

Figure 2-4

I. **Locating Our Scientists**
    A. <u>In Time</u>
    B. <u>In Space</u>
II. **Details About Our Scientists**
    A. <u>Galileo</u> <u>Newton's words</u>
    B. <u>Kepler</u> <u>Newton's words</u>
    C. Descartes Newton's words

Having extra navigation alternatives is always a good idea, and we really wanted to add an example of an outline built with nested ordered lists. (If you didn't create an HTML project with this feature, add one to your own project. Linking anywhere or nowhere is fine as long as you do it in nested, ordered lists, as Figure 2-4 shows.)

We achieved both of our HTML project goals, but in the process we won no prizes for our good looks.

This chapter's project assignment is to use our style sheet to make this outline a great-looking feature. Go Online 2e shows how we did this for our sample project.

Online: Knowits > CSS II > Online > 2 > 2e

And to achieve another teaching goal, please use descendant selectors, not classes.

Quiz

Choose the word or phrase that best completes each sentence.

1) CSS1 was
 a) an official W3C Recommendation in 1996.
 b) never widely supported.
 c) the foundation for all future CSS.
 d) all of the above.

2) The CSS box model areas, inside to outside, are
 a) content, padding, border and margin.
 b) content, margin, border and padding.
 c) content, border, margin and padding.
 d) content, padding, margin and border.

3) CSS box width is measured from
 a) the outside of the box borders.
 b) the inside of the box borders.
 c) the outside of the box content area.
 d) the outside of the box margins.

For questions four through seven, assume that the participating elements
have content, padding, borders and margins.

4) In the rule `#box { top: 0px }` the part of the rule that specifies a
pixel location or locations is
 a) the selector.
 b) the property name.
 c) the property value.
 d) the declaration.

5) In the rule `#box { top: 0px }` top refers to
 a) the top of the content area of #box.
 b) the top of the padding area of #box.
 c) the top of the margin area of #box.
 d) the top of the padding of the container of #box.

6) In the rule `#box { top: 0px }` 0px refers to
  a) the top of the content area of #box's container.
  b) the top of the padding area of #box's container.
  c) the top of the margin area of #box's container.
  d) the top of the border of #box.

7) If the container were the <body> element, the answer to question six
  a) would not change.
  b) would be different.

8) Specifying length in pixels
  a) works well because pixels are always the same size.
  b) does not work because pixels are not always the same size.
  c) works well, although pixels are not always the same size.

9) For a <span> element, the difference between `display:inline-block` and `display:block` is that
  a) the `inline-block` elements are aligned in a neat column.
  b) the `inline-block` elements are placed side-by-side across the page, space permitting.
  c) the `inline-block` elements are aligned, right justified.

10) For a <span> element, the difference between `display:static` and `display:inline` is
  a) none (there is no difference).
  b) `static` displays cannot be moved.
  c) `static` displays are full-width, like `block` displays.

3 Positioning

You started to use positioning when you wrote your first HTML. The `<h1>` heading was on a line by itself. The text and images that came after were "inline" elements, sharing space (if they fit on the line) below the headings. In this chapter we'll explain "normal flow" (the layout that HTML will do without further instructions from your CSS styles) and then show you how to take full control of your pages' layouts.

First, though, a quick look at where we've been.

History

CSS 1 became a W3C Recommendation in December, 1996. The W3C split its HTML group into three parts early in 1997. The part that we are following is the CSS Working Group, which moved at warp speed (for public standards-making processes).

The first CSS 2 standards document was ready in November, 1997. It would become an official W3C Recommendation in May, 1998. As we noted before, it was a *de jure* standard, but it was not a *de facto* standard.

CSS 2 was, however, an important achievement and gave us much that we take for granted today. You've already seen absolute and relative positioning. (They are the subject of this chapter. You needed to use them already just to get your first CSS work completed.) CSS2 also introduced the still-complex subject of z-axis positioning.

CSS 2 provided the first support for media types, including print and aural media. We will refer to print (many users find printed copies helpful, even in today's mobile-saturated world). Aural and other assistive technologies are beyond the scope of this text, but be assured that the CSS you learn here is the CSS used by aural browsers, too. (You don't have `azimuth`—direction to the sound source—on a monitor. But it is just a CSS property used in CSS declarations in aural CSS style sheets.)

CSS 2.1, was the first standard to become a *de facto* standard, years after CSS2. Some CSS 2 ideas were dropped. (CSS 2 had font shadows but they were dropped in CSS 2.1. Do not mourn their loss; they return as a CSS 3 feature and you can use them today.) Most of CSS 2 lives on in today's CSS.

Now, on to positioning.

Normal Flow

As you know, HTML lays out pages for you. It is based on inline and block elements. Many authors just let HTML do the layout without thinking about it. Headings are placed above the text they head. Getting papers on the Web, especially academic papers, doesn't take much markup. From a CSS viewpoint, the layout HTML does is called "normal flow."

Block Elements

In normal flow, the block elements (in HTML5, "block-level" elements) are the easy ones. A block element takes the full width of its container. It is placed below any prior content and above subsequent content. This works perfectly for headings in a text document, for example. (And it is usually just right for block quotes, for numbered and bullet lists and so on.)

Inline Elements

Inline elements are not so simple. First, it may not be obvious that every bit of your content is enclosed in tags separating the elements. You may have `<p>`...`</p>` elements, or you may have text with no visible enclosing tags. If you don't provide the element, CSS specifies an "anonymous" inline-level block element that is wrapped around the text. You cannot style anonymous elements (as there is no way to identify them: no tag, no class, no id).

If you mix elements with text, the individual bits of text are wrapped with anonymous elements. Consider:

```
Lorem <span>text in a span</span> ipsum
```

"Lorem " (space as shown) is wrapped as an anonymous block. And so is " ipsum". In between, your `<span>` forms another, not anonymous, block.

Mostly, but not always, you can forget anonymous blocks and let your browsers handle them. For the "not always" part, try Go Online 3a:

Online: Knowits > CSS II > Online > 3 > 3a

It poses a question. Go Online 3b suggests an answer:

Online: Knowits > CSS II > Online > 3 > 3b

And Go Online 3c makes it conclusive:

Online: Knowits > CSS II > Online > 3 > 3c

(Tempted to skip? Where, in an otherwise empty div, will your browsers (plural) position the bottom of an <img>? It's on the quiz, and should be in your mental toolkit, too.)

Position Property Values

We cover most of the `position` property values here.

`fixed`

A "fixed" element does not scroll with the page. If you want a footer that is always at the bottom of the page, make it `position: fixed`. To be more precise, a fixed element is positioned within the viewport (the window through which the page is viewed) for non-paged media. Normal browser viewing is non-paged. For print media (definitely paged) the element's position is fixed within each output page.

Go Online 3d shows a `position: fixed` header and footer.

Online: Knowits > CSS II > Online > 3 > 3d

`absolute`

An "absolute" position is fixed within its container element. As the container moves, the `position: absolute` element moves with it. With percentage positioning, an absolutely positioned element may also move as its container is re sized. (Is the word "absolute" well-chosen?)

Fixed and absolutely positioned elements are lifted out of normal flow. Other elements are positioned as if they simply did not exist.

Go Online 3e shows a `position:  absolute` header and footer.

Online: Knowits > CSS II > Online > 3 > 3e

`relative`

A "`relative`" position is a location relative to the element's position in normal flow. Positioning properties such as `left` are offsets from the position the browser would otherwise choose. This is often used to make fine adjustments. With `top:-2px` a relatively positioned element is raised a bit.

Go Online 3f shows a `position:  relative` header and footer.

Online: Knowits > CSS II > Online > 3 > 3f

Go Online 3g shows a `position:  fixed` header and footer, above and below a scrolling content area.

Online: Knowits > CSS II > Online > 3 > 3

Positioned Elements

Elements are considered "positioned" if they are `fixed, absolute` or `relative`. Elements are not "positioned" with `static` positions nor are they positioned if the `position` property is not specified. Important: only positioned elements respond to a specified size (`width` or `height`).

If you want to specify the size of an element, but let your browsers otherwise position it in normal flow, specify `position:  relative` and do not specify `left`, `top`, `right` or `bottom`. Your `left` and `top` will default to zero; `right` and `bottom` will be undefined. Without `position:  relative`, your `width` and/or `height` will be ignored and no error will be reported.

Important! When you are varying the `width` or `height` of an element and it refuses to respond that is a sure sign that the element is not positioned.

static

The `position: static` simply specifies that the element will be positioned in normal flow and is not "positioned" when it comes to having a specified size. We have no idea why this is called "static."

Float and Clear Properties

Floated elements may be placed on the left or right side of their containers. Other elements' inline content wraps around them. This is ideal for wrapping text around images. The `clear` property is used in elements that might be pushed out of the way by floated elements. It might more accurately be titled, `do-not-start-until-this-is-in-the-clear`.

float

Wrapping text around an image is very simple. Go Online 3h shows this common use.

Online: Knowits > CSS II > Online > 3 > 3h

That was the simple case: within a single container you were wrapping inline content around an inline element. Unfortunately, you may find your pages needing to float block-level elements, wrapping other inline- and block-level elements around them. This gets more complicated, and quickly.

When you float a block-level element, the element itself does not float. It still takes the full width of its container. The inline elements within the block-level element will wrap around the floated element. The shaded, bordered <p> in Figure 3-1 is an example. Puppy's nose is in front of this <p>. The text within the <p> is floated to the right.

Figure 3-1

Go Online 3i should make this clear.

Online: Knowits > CSS II > Online > 3 > 3i

You can have multiple floated elements on either side. The first one in the markup floats on the side. The second one floats beside the first, and so on. On your own, add another photo to the page you made for Go Online 3i.

Warning: floating elements' height is not recognized by their containing elements. A container with no content other than floats will be zero pixels tall.

clear

The good news about the clear property is that it is very simple. Before CSS, it was an attribute of the HTML <br> tag, such as <br clear='left'>. Add a clear: left declaration to one of the paragraphs floating to the right in your last Go Online to see for yourself.

Display Properties

Setting the display property tells the browser's layout engine how you want an element shown. In scripting it is common to toggle a `div` between `none` and `block`, to hide and show the `div`. (`display: block` is the default for block-level elements, such as `div`s.)

inline

This is the default display for inline-level elements. Seldom specified in CSS, it would be used in scripting to turn an inline-level element on and off. Width, height and margins are not respected.

block

The default for block-level elements. Reminder: block-level elements default to the full width of their containers. Width and height are respected if the block is "positioned." Margins are respected.

inline-block

Changes a block-level element to display like an inline element. Width is reduced to fit the content. Alignment is between other inline elements (space permitting). Width, height and margins are respected.

PPK's Playground

The authoritative "Quirksmode" site, created by Peter-Paul Koch, a long-time frontend engineer and writer based in Amsterdam, includes what he calls a "Playground" where you can set display properties on nested elements. Go there and "play" with the settings until you are confident you understand their interactions.

http://quirksmode.org/css/css2/display.html

list-item

List items are special in that they have a number (ordered) or bullet (unordered) to the left of their content. You may never need to use this display value as it is the default for `<li>` elements.

table-xxx

Their are eight display properties in this group allowing you to replace HTML table-format attributes with CSS rules. Their use is straightforward. To lay out as a `<colgroup>` you would use `display: table-column-group`.

One you should bear in mind is `table-cell`. Vertical alignment works reliably within table cells, but not elsewhere. It is probably a very bad practice to format non-table elements as table cells. On the other hand, if your design requires vertical alignment, this may be the only choice. Sometimes you choose not what is best, but what is least bad.

none

Commonly used in scripting to turn elements on and off, but seldom used in plain CSS (except, possibly, to hide elements that your script will later turn on). There is one key difference between `display: none` and `visibility: hidden` that you should bear in mind.

Using `display: none` deletes your element from the layout, entirely. Using `visibility: hidden` makes your element invisible but places the other elements around it as if it were visible. (This generally leaves an objectionable "hole" in your page. Useful for very unique needs, only.)

Project

We took a good look at our timeline page to see if a little styling would be helpful. You should do the same. You may want to give it a shot before you consider our opinions. These all apply to the timeline page, so an embedded style sheet in that page's <head> was our choice. Here are the improvements we made:

1. We added a border around the table. Pick your own styles.

2. We added some padding inside the table.

3. We created classes for each of our scientists.

4. We defined a background-color for each of our scientist classes (and removed the bg-color=... from the HTML).

5. We created a rule set combining all five of our scientist classes.

6. We used the rule set to add borders (with radii) to all our scientists' table entries.

Of these, removing the bgcolor=... from the HTML is probably most important. We now have the color for Galileo in exactly one place.

When we were happy, we took a new screenshot to replace the old one on the website's home page.

Quiz

Choose the word or phrase that best completes each sentence.

1) CSS2 became an official W3C Recommendation in
    a) 1996.
    b) 1997.
    c) 1998.
    d) 1999.

2) CSS2 was important as
    a) the first true CSS standard.
    b) the foundation for CSS 2.1.
    c) the foundation for CSS 2.1 and current CSS.

3) HTML text
    a) should always be enclosed in blocks.
    b) is enclosed in anonymous blocks.
    c) is enclosed in anonymous blocks if the markup does not enclose it in blocks.

4)Text blocks using different font sizes in normal flow are
    a) aligned on their baselines.
    b) are centered in their blocks.
    c) are an error.

5) Images, in normal flow, are
    a) centered in their lines.
    b) aligned with the top of adjacent text, if any.
    c) aligned with the baseline of adjacent text, if any.
    d) aligned with the default baseline of adjacent text, whether or not there is any adjacent text.

6) Elements that are not part of normal flow are
    a) `static`.
    b) `static` and `relative`.
    c) `fixed` and `absolute`.
    d) `fixed`, `absolute` and `display: none`.

7) A `float: left` element
    a) pushes following elements to its right.
    b) pushes following inline elements to its right.
    c) pushes following text to its right.

8) A `float: left` element following another `float: left` element
    a) is positioned on the container's left, following the earlier `float: left` element.
    b) is positioned to the right of the earlier `float: left` element, space permitting.
    c) is positioned based on the `clear` property of the earlier `float: left` element.

9) For a `<span>` element, the difference between `display:inline-block` and `display:block` is that
    a) the `inline-block` elements are aligned in a neat column.
    b) the `inline-block` elements are placed side-by-side across the page, space permitting.
    d) the `inline-block` elements are aligned, left justified.
    c) the `inline-block` elements are aligned, right justified.

10) To center text vertically
    a) use `vertical-align: center` in the text's element.
    b) use `vertical-align: middle` in the text's element.
    c) use `vertical-align: middle` in the text's containing element.
    d) use `vertical-align: middle` in a `table-cell` container.

4 More Selectors

We've already used selectors, as you can only style what you can select. We've used them to style all HTML elements of a given type, all HTML elements of a given class, and a particular element (by ID). And we've used descendant selectors, to find elements that are enclosed by another element.

Check the link to John Resig's pioneering selector statistics on this chapter's Companion page to see what we're missing.

Online: Knowits > CSS II > Online > 4

Resig's data are from the selectors used with his jQuery library, but their use is very similar to CSS's use of selectors. We've already covered selectors that match over three quarters of those in actual use in Resig's survey of large websites. In this chapter we'll revisit those and add some of the remaining choices. (We'll skip some that are almost never used, and steer you clear of some others you shouldn't use. First, let's look at the rocky road that leads CSS, a good idea but a bit of a caterpillar, to become CSS 2.1, the monarch butterfly we know and love today.

History

A quick timeline:

- Berners-Lee invents WWW, HTML, 1989.
- Mosaic browser (images!), Andreessen and Bina, 1993.
- Lie and Bos present CHSS at Mosaic conference, 1994.
- CSS 1, W3C Recommendation, 17 Dec., 1996
- CSS 2, W3C Recommendation, 12 May, 1998.
- CSS 2.1, W3C Candidate Recommendation, Feb. 25, 2004.
- revert: CSS 2.1, W3C Working Draft, 13 June, 2005.
- CSS 2.1 W3C Candidate Recommendation, 19 July, 2007.
- revert: CSS 2.1, W3C Last Call, Working Draft, 7 December, 2010.
- CSS 2.1, W3C Proposed Recommendation, 12 April, 2011.
- CSS 2.1, W3C Recommendation, 7 June, 2011.

As you can see, it was a "long, strange trip" for CSS 2.1 that began in the last century. The biggest problem limiting wide adoption of CSS was the lack of interoperability between different vendor's version of the tool.

CSS 2.1 was proposed to address interoperability by dropping parts of CSS 2 that were not widely implemented, adopting features that were widely implemented, but not in CSS 2, and attempting to get browser implementers to agree on a true standard. The background for this effort was the "Browser Wars" (originally between Microsoft and Netscape, later between Microsoft and everybody else).

As you might guess, when a Candidate Recommendation is reverted to a Working Draft, it is in serious trouble. CSS 2.1 reverted from CR to WD in 2005, and again in 2010. Those who believed in standards, not just the welfare of a particular corporation, fought doggedly and finally, in 2011, won. We are all indebted to them.

Today we have, in CSS 2.1, a widely interoperable standard. Your styling will be highly compatible from Safari, on the Mac, through Chrome, Firefox and MSIE on Windows (and even on less popular browsers, such as the Blackberry phone's browser or Konqueror on Linux).

Style Sheet Order

Begin your style sheet with "type selectors" (names of HTML tags). Continue with class selectors (they begin with periods). Then follow with ID selectors (they begin with hashes, "#"). When we get to styles' specificity you'll see that this makes the rule very simple: later styles override earlier styles. If your styles are not in this order, the rules are complex.

Within each group, we organize our styles alphabetically. This rule falls apart when you use groups:

```
#top, #right, #bottom, #left { ... }
```

It's better than just hunting, however.

Selector Basics

We start with a quick review, and one selector (that we don't use) which you may see in other people's style sheets.

Universal Selector

The universal selector, an asterisk, styles all element types. If you want to default to 12-point type:

```
* { font-size: 12pt; }
```

We prefer to style the `html` and `body` elements as Listing 4-1 shows:

Listing 4-1

```
html, body {
    font-size: 12pt;
    width: 100%
}
```

You saw the necessity for styling the root element's width in Chapter 3. (You may want to add these styles to your template.)

Simple Selectors

A selector that does not combine with others is called a "simple selector." Listing 4-2 shows examples.

Listing 4-2

```
#one_element { color: red; } /* ID */
p { color: red; } /* type */
.warning { color: red; } /* class */
```

CSS uses the term "type selector" when you style all HTML elements of a given type (tag name).

ID Selectors

You have used ID selectors already and will continue to use them as long as you have CSS styles to assign. We point out here two examples, taken from the W3C CSS 2.1 Recommendation (section 5.9), that you should never follow.

One combines a type with an id: `h1#chapter_1 { … }`. An ID is either unique, or a mistake. `#chapter_1` will get you to the correct element on its own. (There is one fringe case where this combination would make sense. It is so rare that we leave it to you to discover.)

The second is the suggested ID `#z98y`. In the example above, `#chapter_1` is a well-chosen ID (assuming, of course, that it is

assigned to the element starting Chapter 1). `#z98y` is what? All
identifiers should be chosen for their clarity. `#z98y` rates zero on a one-
to-ten clarity scale.

Combinators

A selector is not simple when it combines two (or more) simple selectors
with a combinator (or combinators). You've already used descendant
selectors.

Descendant

A descendant combinator, a simple space, chooses elements (the
descendants) that are enclosed within another selected element. Spans
within paragraphs are selected by `p span`. Go Online 4a shows other
possibilities.

Online: Knowits > CSS II > Online > 4 > 4a

Child

Unlike a descendant selector (which chooses children, grandchildren and
so on), the child combinator selects only immediate children, not
children of children. It is a "greater than" sign: `parent_type >`
`child_type`. Go Online 4b shows child selectors (and how they do not
choose grandchildren).

Online: Knowits > CSS II > Online > 4 > 4b

Grandchild

There is no grandchild combinator, but you can still choose
grandchildren (but not children) with a little creativity. Go Online 4c will
show you how.

Online: Knowits > CSS II > Online > 4 > 4c

Adjacent Sibling

An "adjacent sibling" is one that immediately follows another sibling. The combinator is a plus sign. `ul li + li` chooses the adjacent list item sibling, as shown in Listing 4-3.

Listing 4-3

```
<ul>
    <li> …
    <li> … /* adjacent sibling */
```

Sibling

All the combinators above are specified in CSS 2.1. The "general sibling" is part of CSS 3 and not yet universally available.

A "general" sibling is one that is a sibling of another element (direct descendant of a common parent element), without requiring that it be adjacent. The tilde is the general sibling combinator: `ul ~ li`. Go Online 4d shows adjacent and general siblings.

Online: Knowits > CSS II > Online > 4 > 4d

Attribute Selectors

A type selector (DOM element type) may be further restricted to show only elements that have a specified attribute, and, even further, those with a specified attribute that matches a specified value. These are called "attribute selectors" and they use a special syntax.

Non-Class Attribute Selectors

A selector `type[attribute_name]` chooses all elements of the specified type that have the specified attribute. Looking for floating divs? Use `div[float]`. Looking for divs that float to the right? Use `div[float=right]`.

Class Selectors

If you use divs for right-side sidebar elements, you could create a sidebar class and use a class selector:

```
div.sidebar { /* sidebar declarations */ }
```

That class selector is actually a simplified version of `div[class=sidebar]`, an attribute selector. The class selector version is used more commonly and will be understood by persons without an advanced knowledge of CSS selectors. In general, we would assign classes in the markup (`<div class='sidebar'>`)and use class selectors (`div.sidebar`), rather than attribute selectors. (You may have design elements other than sidebars that also will be chosen by `div[float=right]`).

There is one situation in which we would use attribute selectors: when you do not control the markup. Your markup could be text in a product catalog that will be generated by a PHP program. If you are doing the style sheet, but the HTML comes from an external source, adding classes may not be an option.

Pseudo-Classes

A "pseudo-class" is a set of elements that acts like a class but cannot be placed in a class in the markup. For example, `a:hover` is an `<a>` element over which the mouse hovers. Whether it is a member of the `a:hover` class depends on the viewer's activity with the mouse, not a characteristic that can be known in advance.

Use pseudo-classes at the end of selectors. Use pseudo-class styles after others. If your style for general a elements comes after your style for a:hover elements, the general styles will always be chosen. a:hover must come last.

:first-child

As the name suggests, the first child of each element with child elements will be in the :first-child pseudo-class. We've seen this in other authors' code, but never used it ourselves.

Link :link and :visited

For the viewer, browsers maintain histories and style links that have, and have not, been visited. (Commonly, showing red and blue link colors.) You should seldom, if ever, override the browsers' choices. Your viewers know what their browser's styles mean. How will they know what you mean if you change the default styles?

On occasion, there are very good answers to the above question, however. Don't be afraid to break the rules. Just think carefully before you do.

Dynamic Pseudo-Classes :hover, :active and :focus

In CSS 1 (section 2.1) all the link-related classes were grouped together. CSS 2.1 invented the name "dynamic" (section 5.11.3) to distinguish known-only-during-viewing from other cases. (A link may be :visited from some days ago. A link only becomes :hover when the mouse movement dictates.)

We think that changing the appearance of a link when the mouse is over it is critical to telling the viewer, "Click here and we'll go somewhere!" Our work on the project website (Chapter 2) showed how we do this. Go Online 4e shows it again.

:lang

The `:lang` pseudo-class is either completely unimportant (to most of us) or vital (to some of us). If your pages use multiple languages, you fall in the latter category. Some googling would be well rewarded for you multi-language page authors.

Pseudo-Elements

Pseudo-elements, like pseudo-classes, must follow at the end of selectors. They must also follow selectors for non-pseudo selections.

:first-line and :first-letter

If your web pages are intended to look like antique illuminated manuscripts (the ones monks copied by hand) you will want to be able to provide beautiful drop capitals to start sections. For this you can deal with the `:first-line` and `:first-letter` of a paragraph. They are called "pseudo-elements" as they are only parts of an actual markup element. In the case of `:first-line`, the amount of the paragraph that is part of the pseudo-element is not even known until the page is being laid out.

:before and :after

Like attribute selectors, you should almost always assign classes in the markup rather than use the very rare `:before` and `:after` pseudo-elements. As with attribute selectors, you may have to deal with generated HTML coming from a source you cannot control. These two let you style according to the content of the text an element follows or precedes.

Selector Specificity

The general rule is that the last applicable declaration rules. In a chain, selectors eliminate markup elements, left to right. An `ol` type selector eliminates all elements that are not ordered list elements. An `ol > li` child selector looks first to the parent selection (elements that are ordered lists) and then to the list items that are immediate children of the ordered lists.

If you follow our style sheet order (type selectors, class selectors, id selectors) your selectors will be in specificity order, so the last declaration rules. Consider Listing 4-4.

Listing 4-4

```
a { background-color: gray; }
a:hover { background-color: white; }
```

Your links will have a gray background, unless the mouse pointer is over the link. But consider Listing 4-5.

Listing 4-5

```
a:hover { background-color: white; }
a { background-color: gray; }
```

Your links will always be gray, because that last rule overrides.

You may chain combinators and other selectors as long as you need more specificity. Our grandchild selectors (Go Online 4c) showed one use.

The general rule is an approximation of the real selector specificity rules. This chapter's Companion Page links to the whole truth about selector specificity. It will not be on the quiz. We doubt you'll meet it in your professional work, either.

The normal specificity can be modified by adding `!important` to your CSS declarations. Please never do so. The Companion Page also links to articles explaining why this is a bad idea.

Project

In the lower-left corner of our project home page we have a nested outline of links. The first links are to general pages and the second set is to individual scientists. The scientists' links go to their individual pages, and also to a fragment on the "Newton's Words" page (a bit of lorem ipsum, since Newton wrote Latin).

You should have something similar for this project. (Create it if you haven't got it.) Begin by adding an embedded style sheet to your project home page. Then add a rule that turns the background red for each of these:

- List items (`<li>`) within other list items

- `<a>` links that are children of nested list items

- `<a>` links that are first children of nested list items

- `<a>` links that are adjacent siblings of other `<a>` links within nested list items

View the source of our page if you have trouble. Complete the assignment without matching any of our selectors to prove you really understand!

As we did, comment out all of these unless you think one should be a permanent addition to your project. (Permanent, that is, after you change the declaration to something better than a red background.)

For any of the above, compare the clarity of the selector with a class selector (assuming you added `<xxx class='...'>` to your markup). Would a simple comment in the style sheet be equally clear? Can you choose a class name that makes it more clear?

Quiz

1) `UL LI { declaration(s) }` is an example of:
    a) a child selector.
    b) a descendant selector.
    c) a general sibling selector.
    d) an adjacent sibling selector.

2) CSS 2.1 replaced CSS 2 as a W3C recommendation
    a) after 5 years.
    b) after 8 years.
    c) after 11 years.
    d) after 13 years.

3) All current combinators were specified in CSS 2.1 except for
    a) the grandchild combinator.
    b) the adjacent sibling combinator.
    c) the general sibling combinator.

4) The grandchild combinator
    a) doesn't exist.
    b) can be created with other combinators.
    c) shows one
    good use for the universal selector.
    d) all of the above.

5) Each element in the markup
    a) belongs to a specified class.
    b) may belong to zero or more specified classes.
    c) is assigned to a class.

6) Attribute selectors
    a) select element types that support specific attributes.
    b) select element types that use specific attributes.
    c) select element types that use specific attributes and/or attribute values.

7) A pseudo-class is
    a) a group of elements not defined in the markup.
    b) a way of selecting elements during browser use.
    c) a way of defining links by their use.
    d) all of the above.

8) The `:lang` selector
    a) must come first in a non-simple selector.
    b) is used in multi-language pages.
    c) is a pseudo-element.

9) `:first-letter` and `:first-line` are
    a) used in fancy typography.
    b) pseudo-classes specifying non-standard placements.
    c) advanced combinators.

10) As a general rule you should
    a) use class selectors to avoid the need for advanced selectors.
    b) use attribute selectors only when you have no control over the HTML.
    c) use uncomplicated selectors when they substitute for complicated selectors.
    d) all of the above.

5 More Properties

By now you know how to work with CSS properties. In this chapter we give a very fast tour of all the CSS 2.1 properties, not so that you will memorize them, but so that you will know they exist. There are far too many to memorize. And it is easy to take advantage of the very excellent memories of our search engines.

Beginning in Chapter 6 we will be exploring the future of CSS, including animations and 3D modeling. But first, you want to be able to google for all of CSS 2.1. Your Companion Page:

Online: Knowits > CSS II > Online > 5

has an extensive list of clickable links for the following history.

History

At this point we can take a good look at the W3C's CSS Working Group (aka CSS WG). It was spun out of the HTML group in 1997 (as the CSS & FP Working Group—FP for Formatting Properties) and given its current name in 2000. It has been the group to get all the credit (and blame) for CSS 2, CSS 2.1 and now, CSS 3.

This chapter is the last to focus on CSS 2.1. Next we will be working with CSS 3. (You will see that CSS 3 is vital to getting the most out of CSS, in spite of the fact that there really is no such thing as CSS 3. We hope minor contradictions don't bother you.)

The CSS WG works today on Modules of specifications. CSS 2.1 was the last everything-in-one-document standard. The modules follow a more-or-less organized process. First, we have a proposal, then the proposal is embodied in a Working Draft (WD). This may get shot down, revised beyond recognition or it may successfully march along the standards path.

For a proposal to succeed, the WD will start as an Exploring document; graduate to Rewriting (major revisions here); continue with Revising and Refining (progressively working from major concepts to minor details). Nearing completion, the editor(s) issues a Last Call and the standard finally achieves Stable status as a Candidate Recommendation. When the last "i" is dotted, the WG issues a Proposed Recommendation which will be kicked upstairs in the W3C, checked for having its paperwork in good order and finally be issued as a W3C Recommendation.

At or before the Candidate Recommendation (Stable) stage, vendors will be busy adding the new features to their browsers and we frontend engineers will begin to use the new features (praying that the final changes do not destroy our beautiful pages).

Beginning in Chapter 6, we will be paying close attention to the exact stage of each CSS 3 feature in the CSS WG process. For now, however, we take a final look at CSS 2.1's complete set of properties.

The companion page's first link is to Appendix F (full property table) of the CSS 2.1 Recommendation. It features an alphabetic list of all properties. Each property is linked to its formal definition in the Recommendation. You may want to have Appendix F open in at least one browser tab whenever you work with CSS. (The standard is far more readable than most technical documents.)

All Media

Some properties are specific to visual media. Colors make no sense to an aural browser, reading web pages to its "viewers." Other properties make sense in other media. A few properties, which we cover here, are applicable to all media. For example, `display: none` will make an element hide, regardless of media (in spite of the fact that the name suggests a visual property).

We organize these properties by media type (last column in the official table): all media, aural and visual media. Within the visual media properties we group the visual-only first, then the visual/interactive media, and last, the visual/paged media. Grouping within the visual-only is our topical organization. You can follow this on:

Online: Knowits > CSS II > Outlines > Properties

content

You can add content to `:before` and `:after` pseudo elements. Go Online 5a shows this.

Online: Knowits > CSS II > Online > 5 > 5a

counter-

The trailing hyphen indicates that this topic is part of a set of property names, in this case `counter-increment` and `counter-reset`.

Counters can automatically increment. In combination with the content property, these could automatically number the sections in a technical paper.

```
display
```

See Chapter 3, "Display Properties."

Aural Media

An aural browser (often called a "reader") speaks to a visually impaired site visitor. For a list of the aural properties, begin with our property list:

Online: Knowits > CSS II > Outlines > Properties

Expand the "Aural" topic. Then use the official Appendix F to learn more.

Warning: The CSS3 "speech" media replaces the CSS 2.1 "aural" media and makes many significant changes. Proceed with caution.

Visual Media Only

This group of properties excludes those that combine visual/interactive media and visual/paged media. We group the visual-only properties into six sub-groups.

Background

If you are using our outline, you see both background and background- subtopics. This lets you know that there is a background shorthand property that lets you combine individual background-xxx properties.

The background-xxx properties include attachment, color, image, position and repeat.

If you have the opportunity to use a background image (picture) you can explore here. Your image will be centered and repeated (or not) horizontally and vertically. Or it will be positioned as you specify. You can "attach" it to the viewport (like `position: fixed`) or let it scroll with the canvas.

Note: The standard refers to the "URI" of resources such as images. This was, formerly, subtly different from URL. The difference was so slight that few understood it and eventually it was dropped. Use URLs where the standard specifies URIs.

This chapter's Project work explores backgrounds further.

Border

Our properties outline lists the "four sides" subtopic. That is our shorthand for `border-xxx`, `border-left-xxx`, `border-top-xxx`, `border-right-xxx` and `border-bottom-xxx` properties (where xxx is a border property suffix such as `color`, `style` or `width`).

The border property is a convenient shorthand when you don't want to style the sides individually. This is a common specification: `border: 1px solid black`. We are partial to `border: green solid 1px` during development. (No, we've never seen a single-pixel, green border on the web. That's precisely why we use it during development. You obviously won't leave it unchanged before you put your page online.)

Go Online 5b shows how far you can, and cannot, go in exploiting all the border possibilities.

Online: Knowits > CSS II > Online > 5 > 5b

If you have been following the W3C Appendix F you know that we have not discussed `border-collapse`. This is included in the next section as a table-related property.

Other

Here we have collected those visual-only properties that do not fit into one of our subtopics.

`auto`

Divs and other block-level elements default to `auto` height and width. That means tall enough to fit the content and the full width of the viewport or other container. This is normally the size you want. Note that `100%` (the width of the container) is seldom what you want. This gives the element's content area `100%` of the width of the container. The overall width of the element will be `100%` plus the `padding`, plus the `border` and the `margin`. That means scrolling will be required, in most cases. The `auto` width adjusts the element's content size so that the element, with padding, borders and margin, will just fit its container. (Note: the new CSS3 `box-sizing: border-box` declaration almost, but not quite, makes `100%` a sensible width. See Chapter 7, Basic UI.)

`clip`

At present, you can "clip" (as in cropping a photograph) text within a rectangle. You can also use a simple div to define the clipping area, which will be readily understood by the next programmer assigned. This property may become important with the CSS 3 shapes module, which will permit clipping to multiple shapes. We are avoiding it for now.

`List-` and `Table-` Related

There are a series of properties for specialized work with lists and tables. We invite you to explore them on your own when you want to create great styles for either lists or tables. (Use the other styles if you can. Few will know these properties.)

visibility

A reminder: `visibility: hidden` is not like `display: none`. The latter makes an element disappear. The former leaves a hole in your layout the size of the hidden element. (This is a favorite job interview question, even though `visibility: hidden` is almost never useful.)

Position

This was the subject of Chapter 3. Here are some reminders.

`position`

In a truly inexplicable decision, the CSS WG determined that if you omit the position property, failing to create a "positioned" element, your size specifications will be ignored. Position must be `fixed`, `absolute` or `relative` or your `height` and `width` don't matter.

`left` / `top` and `bottom` / `right`

You position the `top-left` corner, commonly. You replace one or both of these with `bottom` and/or `right`, rarely. You must not specify `left` and `right`, nor `top` and `bottom`.

`float` / `clear`

You `float` elements `left` or `right` when you want text to wrap around them. Remember: the floated element does not push other elements out of the way. The floated element pushes text and other inline-level elements out of the way.

`vertical-align`

The vertical-align property is almost completely ignored unless you specify `display: table-cell`.

`z-index`

Higher z-indices are closer to the viewer (in front of and hiding elements with lower z-indices) but only within the same "stacking context." The stacking context rules are so complex that we always try to place the elements that we want in front to come after (in the markup) elements that we want to (partially) hide.

Size

This was one of the subjects of Chapter 2. Again, some reminders.

height / width

The `height` and `width` properties apply only to positioned, block-level elements. Remember this fact when your size specifications are being ignored.

max- / min-

You may specify `max-height` and `max-width`, and / or `min-height` and `min-width`. These are especially important when you create fluid and responsive layouts (Chapter 6).

margin / padding

You may specify a single value for `margin` and `padding`. These apply to all four sides. You may also append a side suffix, one of `-left`, `-top`, `-right` or `-bottom`, to specify the value for that side. You may also specify four values without adding the size suffix. These apply clockwise from the top. Standards are also provided for two- and three-value specifications, but using individual sides will be much more readable. (First rule for good coding: never show off!)

Text-Related

HTML was rooted in the need to share documents that were primarily, or entirely, text. It should be no surprise that CSS provides extensive properties for text.

color

The `color` property specifies the color of the foreground elements, primarily text. (The `background-color` is the one you want to color the whole element.) Other foreground elements include list bullets and horizontal rules.

direction

For western languages, the default left-to-right direction may be all you need. For Semitic languages (such as Arabic and Hebrew) you may need to specify `direction: rtl` and `direction: ltr` if your document uses both. You will need to google for more information on these and for east Asian languages.

font

You have already used font properties in following the Go Online "Your Turn" assignments. These include `font-family`, `font-size`, `font-style` and `font-variant`. As the values are all unique, you may combine them in the shorthand font property: `font: 12pt Arial bold`.

For the font family (a comma-separated list, in descending order of your preference) we would recommend always using one of `sans-serif`, `serif`, `monospace` or `cursive`, as the standard specifies. This lets the browser select its recommended family. Unfortunately, MSIE's choice of default `serif` font is so bad that you really must specify one. `'Times New Roman'` is a good, general-purpose choice. You must put the family name in quotes if it includes spaces.

`'Courier New'`, the usual monospace default, is a good one except that it confuses the lowercase letter "l" and the numeral "1". No browser correctly chooses a cursive font family if you ask for `cursive`. The standard also specifies a `fantasy` font default. No browser chooses something that could reasonably be called a `fantasy` fault.

letter-spacing

In general, the browsers all choose letter spacing to achieve the best possible result for your viewers, and they do it well. Non-standard choices will probably be worse. If you are an expert in the typography field, ignore this advice and suit yourself. Default spacing may not be satisfactory when you rotate text (Chapter 9). You may need to add a pixel or two between letters for legibility after a rotation.

`letter-spacing: 1px;` adds an extra pixel between letters.

line-height

Like `letter-spacing`, `line-height` will be chosen by the browser. Also like `letter-spacing`, you should probably let the browsers choose unless you have considerable expertise. One exception: to center a single word or line of text in an element, without using `display: table-cell`, set the `line-height` to twice the element's height.

Unlike most lengths, `line-height` can be specified as a unitless number: `1.25`, for instance. This is applied as a ratio to computed `font-size`, which will give a good result for text, headings, lists and other elements. The standard recommends the use of unitless line height.

quotes

We have seen lots of web pages that made quite a mess with HTML and/or CSS by trying to ensure correctly matched true quotes. (The vertical ones are correctly called "inch marks" and "apostrophes". Ones that curl left and right, as in the last sentence, are true quotes.)

Your first choice should be HTML, not CSS. Use the `<q>` and `</q>` tags around quotes. HTML will use the page's language to select the appropriate symbols.

Unfortunately, not all browsers are smart enough (more accurately, well-programmed enough) to correctly nest quotes. If you must get this right, click on the "quotes" property in Appendix F of the standard. The example in the standard, showing how to combine Norwegian and English quoting, is exceptionally clear. Go Online 5c helps you try it yourself.

Online: Knowits > CSS II > Online > 5 > 5c

text-

There are four text-related properties that start with the "text-" prefix: `text-align`, `text-decoration`, `text-indent` and `text-transform`.

You may align your text to the `left`, `center`, `right` or `justify`. Western languages default to `left`. It is easy to create bad designs using `center`. Use `right` (or `left`, if your language reads right-to-left) as needed. When it was new, `justify` was popular as it looked like the text in books. With apologies to the expert typographers, and typesetting programs that emulated them, `justify` is almost never used today because it is almost always harder to read.

If you never decorate your text you will be doing well. Browsers commonly underline links. If you don't underline links except when we hover over them, we'll like your pages. If you are sharing documents among multiple editors, you may want to use underlines, overlines and strike-throughs. Blink was abandoned almost twenty years ago as one of the really bad ideas in the history of the web.

You can combine `text-indent` with the `:first-line` pseudo element if you like old-fashioned typewritten documents. You can use `text-transform` if you like SHOUTING.

unicode-bidi

The "bidi" is short for bi-directional. You might write an English word or computer program source code (or CSS rules) left-to-right in a right-to-left language document. We leave it to you to google for more complex bi-directional overrides and for HTML5's `<bdi>` tag. (As always, ask **caniuse.com** about new tags.)

white-space

The CSS declarations `white-space: pre` and `white-space: normal` can be used in lieu of the HTML `<pre>` and `</pre>` elements. Similarly, `white-space: nowrap` could be used in a `<span>` in lieu of `<nobr>` and `</nobr>`.

word-spacing

The value following the word-spacing property is the amount of space to be added to the normal spacing. Before you let a well-intentioned designer insist on a particular spacing for his or her headline, be sure you ask, "In which browser?" Normal spacing depends on the font, alignment, letter spacing and browser, so adding a pixel or two may not achieve "pixel perfect" except in one browser, for one device. Also, if we haven't scared you away, you may use negative amounts.

Visual and Other Media

We now move on to the properties (far fewer!) that apply to both visual and other media. The "other" that share this distinction are "interactive" and "paged" media.

Visual and Interactive Media

cursor

The common browser behavior is to change from `cursor: default` to `cursor: pointer` when the mouse pointer is over a link. (The "pointer" is not the default arrow, it is the hand with the pointing finger.) The text cursor (an I-beam) also will alternate with the default cursor as your mouse pointer moves over most pages.

Remember that fingers, not mice, are the pointers on smaller devices while you look at Go Online 5d, which covers mouse cursors.

online: Knowits > CSS II > Online > 5 > 5d

Pay attention to the cursors which are available (fewer than CSS specifies). Also note those which are merely twins (`n-resize`, `ns-resize`). Note that even a tiny sample of `cursor: none` is confusing.

CSS also specifies cursors loaded from URL's though loading tiny graphics is usually not a good idea (up to a third of a second extra for loading each cursor), and CSS specifies `cursor:  inherit`, which we have never seen in practice.

outline, outline-

An outline is a border, modified for use during development. Unlike a border, it does not occupy pixels. It wraps tightly around text and other anonymous blocks.

Visual and Paged Media

orphans, widows

In typesetting, an "orphan" is a paragraph's first line by itself at the bottom of a page. Similarly, a "widow" is a paragraph's last line by itself at the top of a page. (Warning: These definitions are often reversed.) The values of the `orphan` and `widow` properties specify the minimum number of lines to be left at the bottom and top of the page. The default value is 2.

At least, the default value will be 2 when the browsers implement this feature. Despite the fact that this is a CSS 2.1 property, it is not widely implemented. You can, (November, 2013) use CSS 3 multi-column layouts (`column-count:  2`) but when you do you will quickly see the need for orphan and widow control.

Sorry to say, your need is not yet met. Go Online 5e lets you test in your own browsers.

online: Knowits > CSS II > Online > 5 > 5e

page-break-

The `page-break-` properties are another CSS 2.1 idea that is not yet implemented. It has limited value until we get orphan and widow control.

We keep watching for it, hoping to have heading tags (e. g., <h2>) not land at the bottom of one column while the material they head starts the next column. Actually, `page-break-after: avoid` should be the default for headings.

Project

At this point you have a sound background in traditional CSS, including almost all of CSS 2.1. This time the project is for you to apply your new savvy to improve your site.

Set a simple goal: three improvements.

We recommend a critical look at each of your pages. Which one most needs help? What one bit of style will do the most for it?

And when you have improved the worst page, go back to the previous paragraph. Hopefully, the page you just worked on is no longer your site's worst. Repeat the mandate of the previous paragraph a total of three times. Or more.

You should be looking at first-rate work before you go on.

Quiz

1) The CSS Working Group (CSS WG) was formed in
   a) 1997, as the CSS and FP Working Group.
   b) 2000, as the CSS Working Group (CSS WG).
   c) both of the above.

2) CSS 3 is
   a) the planned successor to CSS 2.
   b) the planned successor to CSS 2.1.
   c) an informal name for new CSS modules.

3) The CSS 2.1 properties that apply to all media are:
   a) `content`, `counter-` and `display`.
   b) `content`, `counter-increment` and `cursor`.
   c) `content`, `counter-increment`, `counter-reset`. and
   `display`.
   d) `content`, `counter-increment`, `counter-reset` and
   `cursor`.

4) Aural media properties include
   a) `altitude`, `pitch`, `richness` and `voice`.
   b) `azimuth`, `elevation`, `stress` and `volume`.
   c) `cue`, `pause`, `pitch` and `value`.
   d) `cue`, `depth`, `elevation` and `stress`.

5) The correct order for the border shorthand is
   a) `border: green 1px solid`.
   b) `border: 1px solid green`.
   c) `border: solid green 1px`.
   d) any of the above.

6) You would use `visibility: hidden` to
   a) leave empty spaces in your pages.
   b) answer job-interview questions.
   c) both of the above.

7) The `vertical-align` property is used to
   a) put equal whitespace above and below any element in a div.
   b) put equal whitespace above and below text in a div.
   c) vertically center content in a `display: block` element.
   d) vertically center content in a `display: table-cell` element.

8) Specifying `width` is appropriate for
   a) `position: relative` and `position: fixed` elements.
   b) `position: static` elements.
   c) unpositioned and `position: absolute` elements.
   d) none of the above.

9) Color is
   a) a background property.
   b) a text property.
   c) an aural media property.

10) Entering and leaving a link the cursor commonly changes
   a) from `normal` to `text`.
   b) from `default` to `text`.
   c) from `default` to `pointer`.
   d) from `pointer` to `default`.

6 Multi-Device Pages

While the CSS standard has helped simplify life for people who create web pages, the incredible proliferation of web-enabled devices has certainly made frontend engineers lives more complicated. We used to worry about the size of the monitor attached to our viewer's PC. Now we wonder if our viewer is using a smartphone, tablet, notebook, laptop, PC or maybe a wrist watch, eyeglasses, game console or car dashboard.

Let's take a quick look back at devices that have been and are being used.

History

So far our histories have been focused on software. For this chapter we will look at hardware's history. Specifically, the history of display devices.

Before the PC, video monitors hooked to mainframe computers were known as "3270" or "green screen" terminals. IBM manufactured a line of terminal equipment (the terminals, controllers and other communications components) whose part numbers were 327x. The terminals themselves were 3277s. The original Model 1 (1971) displayed 12 lines, 40 characters each of green text on a black screen. The most popular, Model 2, upgraded to 24 lines of 80 characters each. (80 characters was the width of the then ubiquitous punch cards, a width that is still commonly used for programming.)

The first popular personal computer, the Apple II, had no monitor. It was connected to external monitors including color TVs (very low resolution) and character-based monochrome screens, mostly 24 line, 80 characters, some using the same green phosphors that the 3277 used.

Personal computers became hugely popular in business with the introduction of the IBM PC. For applications such as word processing, you needed an MDA card (Monochrome Display Adapter) hooked to a monitor such as the ones used with the Apple II. This added an extra line to achieve 25x80 text. You could use a CGA (Color Graphics Adapter) to hook to a color television (very poor resolution) or color monitor showing 320x200 pixels of 16-color graphics, or 24 lines of 40 character text (suitable for labels on charts, but not for word processing). A truly high-end system used Lotus 1-2-3 showing a spreadsheet on an MDA monitor and simultaneous color charts on a CGA monitor.

IBM led the way in PCs during the '80s, steadily improving everything including its graphics adapters. The Enhanced Graphics Adapter (EGA, 1984) was followed by the modestly named Video Graphics Adapter (VGA, 1987). The VGA standard began with 640x480, 256-color graphics and 50 line, 80 character text. For the first time a single monitor could support both graphic and text applications.

In the '90s, IBM's leadership was challenged and the market fragmented. Competition gave us SVGA graphics (Super, 800x600), then XGA (eXtended, 1024x768). Many websites are still designed for XGA monitors.

Market leadership, if not control, returned to Apple in 2007 with the introduction of the iPhone and was reinforced in 2010 with the introduction of the first major tablet, the iPad. Today we have a continuum of devices with manufacturers trying to supply every size and budget.

Phones less than 200 pixels wide proliferated after the original iPhone but are rapidly fading from the market. Large smartphones now boast resolutions that were formerly desktop monitor sizes: Apple 4s is 640x960; Nokia Lumia 800 is 480x800; Google Nexus is 720x1280. Pixel density varies from 252 ppi—about 100 ppcm—for the Nokia to 330 for the Apple.

Desktop monitors (and large TVs) are popular at 1080p (1920x1080) resolution. New "Quad HD" (QHD, 2560x1440) monitors are now available for moderate prices. "4K UHD" (3840x2160) still cost thousands of dollars but may cost only hundreds of dollars by the time you read this. (1080p at 446 ppi is also available in a smartphone, today, for those who really love their pixels. The best tablets can exceed all normal desktop monitors in pixel dimensions.)

What does history tell us about the future? That today's lowest resolution phones will be gone soon. That even smaller devices (wearable) will be here soon. And that larger devices (larger in physical size and in pixels) will be available on desktops, soon.

Design for Width

To simplify, we recognize that viewers with smaller devices are accustomed to scrolling vertically, but they are not happy scrolling horizontally. (Except in east Asia, text is read top-to-bottom, so clicking or swiping "page down" reveals the next block of text." Readers who create pages for east Asian languages will have to adjust this discussion.)

Our challenge is to make our content fit in the width of the viewer's device.

First we need to decide which devices we want to support. An information site, such as our sample projects, would commonly be viewed on a desktop or laptop computer. It would be nice if it could support tablets, too. Phones? Perhaps we want to show phones a page that tells them what our site is about and encourages them to view it on a wider screen.

Note that this is not a recommendation that would be good for your local pizza parlor. They may get most of their online business from viewers using phones. Your decision on device sizes must be to support the devices your viewers actually use, not to support the devices that you wish they would use.

Also, you must bear in mind that even a dictum as simple as "design for width" is simple to say, but not so simple to follow. Tablets and phones are commonly made to change orientation from portrait to landscape as the user turns them 90 degrees. An ideal page changes its layout to reflect the change in orientation. (And don't worry if your pages are less than ideal. Very few pages can accommodate this change.)

Fluid Design

"Fluid" design means layout that gracefully adapts to different widths. HTML was designed to provide fluid layout, by default. Headings default to full-width blocks so they come above the content they head. Text blocks wrap their content to fit their container. The idea was to support devices of different widths, right from the birth of the web.

Today you can carry fluid principles much further. Headings and other text can be displayed at device-appropriate sizes. (Phones and tablets are held much closer to the eyes than desktop monitors, so you can use smaller text.) Graphics can be sized in proportion to the viewing area.

Responsive Design

Responsive design was named and promoted by Ethan Marcotte, beginning with an article in the web design eZine, *A List Apart* (May, 2010, clickable link on the Companion Page) and followed by his 2011 book, *Responsive Web Design*. The iPhone and iPad, and their competitors, were rapidly changing the way viewers looked at the web, but many sites were slow to respond. Marcotte advocated sites that could handle a wide range of devices.

While fluid design changes sizes of your content to fit smaller (or larger) devices, responsive design also adjusts the layout to better fit the device, often using flexible grids. This may be as simple as moving a navigation bar from the left margin to the top. Labels for graphics may be moved from beside the graphic to below the graphic.

More fundamental rearrangements may be made. Two content areas may be changed from side-by-side to over-and-under for smaller devices. Text sidebars may be moved into the vertical flow.

Post-Responsive Design

While responsive design attempts to bring content to a wider range of devices, more recent design types advocate tailoring the content, not just the layout, to fit different devices. Names such as "content-driven" design, "responsive experience" and "adaptive design" have been promoted, though none have caught on widely.

The principle is sound. If viewers visiting your site with phones have different needs than viewers using desktop computers, they should be served content appropriate to their needs.

At-Rules

Unlike regular CSS rules (selectors followed by declarations) the at-rules all start with an "@" sign. They control CSS, not the presentation of elements on the page. One, @media, is vital for responsive designs. This is a partial list of at-rules.

@import

If you use one, the @import rule (or rules—you may use as many as you like) must begin your CSS. It imports another CSS external stylesheet into the current one. You specify a stylesheet using either a pseudo-function URL notation, or as a string. Listing 6-1 shows both.

Listing 6-1

```
@import url( "support/another.css" );
@import "styles/my_styles.css";
```

Go Online 6a shows how these are done.

Online: Knowits > CSS II > Online > 6 > 6a

You may also specify media types (tv or mobile for examples) for your imported stylesheets.

@charset

Important to international enterprises, the @charset rule lets you specify the character set of the current stylesheet. It should precede everything except @import rules.

@font-face

We leave you to research this on your own. If your designer insists on a particular font, the @font-face rule lets you import a font that your viewers might not have on their devices. (In many cases we would question whether this is enough of a benefit to justify the extra download time.)

@keyframes

@keyframes let you specify rules to apply at fixed points during an animation. Details are in Chapter 10.

@media

Go Online 6b shows the implementation of separate styles for screen and print media.

Online: Knowits > CSS II > Online > 6 > 6b

Media queries (@media rules with conditionals) are the subject of the next section.

@page

Used for print output, the @page rule lets you define :first, :left and :right pages. (This book uses that formatting scheme. Note the position of the page numbers: bottom right on each chapter's first page, then at top left and top right on alternating pages within each chapter.)

Media Queries

The CSS WG began working on CSS subsets before CSS 2.1 was finished. Efforts to create standards for TV and mobile subsets, for examples, have not succeeded. The hardware has advanced faster than the standards-making process. The one media standard that is widely used is the print standard, commonly used to format pages in a printer-friendly style.

But with the addition of conditionals, @media rules have become fundamental to responsive and post-responsive design techniques.

@media with Conditionals

The screen media type simply identifies a browser with a visual display. That includes the smallest smartphone, the highest resolution tablet, the largest desktop and more. Conditional expressions let you provide CSS based on device widths, orientation (portrait or landscape) and more.

You can provide separate styles within a stylesheet for a selected range of widths, or you can provide separate stylesheets for different width ranges. You can also vary styles based on many other characteristics, including display height and orientation (portrait or landscape).

Go Online 6c begins with the creation of a set of "ruler" divs, that let you check your media queries.

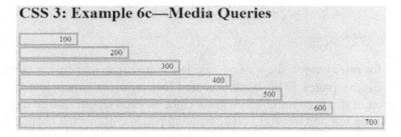

Figure 6-1

The the Go Online has you create styles set for a range of widths. You'll see these work as you drag your browser's sides in and out.

Online: Knowits > CSS II > Online > 6 > 6c

Testing with Emulators

You test your work in Go Online 6c by simply dragging your browsers borders in and out. A much better test, of course, is to view your work on a variety of devices. However, maintaining just a complete set of iPhones is now a very expensive proposition. Maintaining even an incomplete set of multiple vendors phones and tablets is beyond the means of any but the best financed labs. (Consider, perhaps only briefly, the budget needed for testing car dashboard browsers.)

One partial solution to this problem is the software emulator. With an emulator, you can view your work as it should look on any of a wide variety of devices with just your desktop monitor. See the chapter 6 Companion Page's links for a good choice of (mostly free) emulators including phones, tablets and gaming devices. (If your budget permits you may want to google for paid services.)

Project

Now we turn to your project site. If you built yours while learning HTML we assume you were working on a content-creation device (desktop or laptop). Open your site in your favorite browser(s) and drag the right edge toward the left for a quick, multi-device test. You'll probably see lots of issues. Our sample site had lots of issues.

Your project, from here through the end of this knowit, is to make your site multi-device capable. We will be making ours more fluid, varying layout as needed and varying content as required. Our first challenge is to study our viewers and find out what they want. Absent a budget for hiring a marketing firm to help us, we'll make some assumptions.

Market Assessment

Ours is an information site. Our viewers want to learn about 17th century scientists. We assume they have something bigger than a phone. (And where possible, we'll make our pages fit phones, too.) We'll try to be appropriate for anything from a good tablet to a large desktop device.

Site Analysis

After you decide what devices to support, you have to look at your site to see where it needs work. Some issues (navigation, for one) effect most or all pages. Others are specific to individual pages. On our project we found these issues:

- All – top menu gets ugly at small sizes, requires too much space
- All – `<h1>` element is too big for smaller devices
- All – text is the same size on all devices
- All – text is too wide for reading on wider devices

- Home – five-abreast portraits require horizontal scrolling
- Home – timeline/map should be over/under on narrow devices
- Home – bottom outline nav fails on very narrow devices
- Timeline needs horizontal scrolling below desktop widths
- Map page same as timeline page
- Individual scientists – OK when 'All' issues fixed
- 'Newton said' – 'text too wide' very important here
- Credits – same issue as Home page portraits

Your project for this chapter is to think through the market for your project site and decide what devices your viewers will want you to support. Then, do your site analysis. Go through your pages and list the improvements they need. Last, make a plan.

Site Plan

Does your site support every device equally well? Hardly likely. You need two things to make a plan. First, you need the site analysis. What needs to be done? Second, you need a budget.

Your budget is the amount of time you can afford to spend working on your site for each of the remaining chapters in this knowit. Will a half hour per chapter get the job done? Can you afford two hours per chapter?

Then, based on the analysis and your budget you can set priorities and make a schedule. Don't be afraid to decide against items you found in your analysis. If you can't get everything done within your budget, make sure you get the most important things done.

And be sure you work your schedule. Before you complete the Chapter 7 Quiz, complete your Chapter7 site improvements. Or complete as much as you can and reschedule the rest. Don't leave yourself unpleasant surprises for Chapter 10.

To view our site before we made it multi-device capable, visit the HTML version at:

Online: Knowits > HTML I > Project

The multi-device version:

Online: Knowits > CSS II > Project

(Almost all changes were done in the stylesheet, not the HTML.)

You may want to look at the Project topics in the next four chapters to see how we divided our time among the items on our list. You might be facing very similar issues.

Quiz

1) The screen resolution of visual devices
   a) is rapidly diverging for multiple devices types.
   b) is rapidly converging one one standard.
   c) is steadily increasing.
   d) is independent of device orientation.

2) The first major "smartphone," the Apple iPhone was introduced in
   a) 2001.
   b) 2003.
   c) 2005.
   d) 2007.

3) The first popular tablet, the Apple iPad, was introduced in
   a) 2006.
   b) 2008.
   c) 2010.
   d) 2012.

4) "1080p" screen resolution is available in
   a) large TVs.
   b) TVs, desktop monitors and smartphones.
   c) TVs and desktop monitors.

5) Pages should be designed for width
   a) when the language's block flow is vertical.
   b) when the device is in portrait orientations.
   c) when the language's inline flow is vertical.
   d) when width is best for images.

6) Unlike fluid design, responsive design
   a) adjusts the layout of elements based on device size.
   b) permits the use of different devices.
   c) resizes elements based on overall width.
   d) tailors font sizes for viewing distances.

7) CSS at-rules are named for
    a) their starting character.
    b) their location at the top of the page.
    c) the syntax of import rules.

8) Media may be specified in
    a) media at rules.
    b) import at rules.
    c) media queries.
    d) all of the above.

9) Print stylesheets may
    a) specify font and other sizes.
    b) specify colors.
    c) specify alternate background images.
    d) specify all styles, including display.

10) Conditional expressions may be used to
    a) specify maximum devices widths.
    b) specify minimum devices widths.
    c) style separately for portrait and landscape orientation.
    d) all of the above.

7 CSS 3 Modules

The W3C CSS Working Group discovered that a single, monolithic CSS specification was no longer practical during the CSS 2 to CSS 2.1 journey (13 years between official standards). To allow work to proceed at Internet speed, the WG split the project into Modules that could be completed independently. Today we have many modules officially at Level 3 and even a handful working on Level 4. "CSS 3" is not the name of a standard, it is the collective name for the CSS Level 3 Modules.

In this chapter we'll look at all the Level 3 Modules that have advanced to Recommendation, Candidate Recommendation and Last Call (Working Draft) status. And we'll mention a few others which we are eager to see moving toward completion.

History

As always, see the Companion Page for clickable links. And thank "fantasai" for much of this history.

The plan to modularize CSS was first made public in 2000 with the publication of "CSS 3 Introduction" by the CSS & FP Working Group. "FP" (Formatting Properties) would be dropped from the group name later in 2000.

The original plan was to have a series of "core" modules augmented by other, detailed modules. As this created unwanted dependencies (detailed modules could not be completed until the core modules were completed) the core modules were dropped. In their place, CSS 2.1 (which itself was years from completion) was established as the base. Level 3 modules were to expand on CSS 2.1 but not to modify it.

The 2000 plan would be updated in 2007 with the "Beijing" Snapshot, the first of a planned series of informative status reports on the work in progress, listed by module. Beijing formalized the decision to build on CSS 2.1 (and all but discarded CSS 2, though it was a formal Recommendation while CSS 2.1 was still not formally approved).

Beijing also included the "Profiles" (Print, TV and Mobile) which were to provide subsets of CSS applicable to less powerful hardware. These profiles may be extinct by the time you read this, a fate not uncommon in the history of slow-moving public standards being defined for fast-moving technology.

The 2010 Snapshot updates Beijing. The rest of this chapter brings the history forward to late 2013.

Recommendations

Recommendations are official W3C standards and should be followed by all browsers. (The key word here is "should." Microsoft deliberately avoids updating IE8 on Windows XP, for example, and does not support CSS 3 in IE8. So you cannot assume that a CSS3 Recommendation is

available to all your potential viewers. As with HTML, check
caniuse.com for the latest status of any style declaration.)

Color

The color standard now provides the `opacity` property (long-supported
in non-Microsoft browsers). Its value is a number from 0.0 (transparent)
through 1.0 (opaque).

The color standard also provides the `rgba` pseudo-function notation for
color values: `rgba( 0, 255, 255, 0.5 )` is cyan, 50% opaque.
You may use percentages for the colors, but not the alpha component. Go
Online: `rgba( 0%, 100%, 100%, 0.5)` is the same 50% opaque
cyan.

There is, unfortunately, no rgba alternative in hexadecimal. We would
much prefer to type `#00ffff88` or, for minimalists, `#0ff8`. (We'll be
patient. The W3C has added four- and eight-digit hex values to the Level
4, aka CSS 4, specification.)

For those with a print background, the HSL alternative is supported (hue,
saturation and lightness). If you know print, you may have called the "L"
"luminance." The notation is again a pseudo-function: `hsl(h,s,l)` or
`hsla(h,s,l,opacity)`.

Go Online 7a illustrates amounts of transparency.

Online: Knowits > CSS II > Online > 7 > 7a

Go Online 7b, built on the same code as Go Online 7a, illustrates the
sometimes daunting challenge of achieving cross-browser compatibility.
If you can complete this challenge, frontend engineering may be your
career. (Warning: frontend guru Douglas Crockford calls the browser "a
really hostile programming environment." This is what he means.)

Online: Knowits > CSS II > Online > 7 > 7b

Note: Opacity applies to the element, including all its children. Background color opacity applies only to the background color. An image on a 50% opaque background (`rgba(r,g,b, 0.5)`) is still an opaque image. An image on a div that is `opacity: 0.5` will be 50% opaque. See the carousel, Appendix A, for an example of translucent images in motion.

Namespaces

There is a namespace standard useful in conforming CSS to XHTML for those who require XML compatibility.

Selectors

Additions to CSS 2.1 selectors are relatively modest. Pseudo-classes now include "user action" ("dynamic" in 2.1) classes. These are `:hover`, `:active` and `:focus`. This module also defines "UI element states" classes: `:enabled`, `:disabled`, `:checked`, and `:indeterminate`.

A large group of "structural pseudo-classes" has been added such as `:root`, `:nth-child()` and `:first-child` and `:nth-last-of-type()`. We refer you to the links on the companion page for more information regarding these. We also caution against use of these uncommon selectors if there are other alternatives (such as providing sensibly named classes).

One interesting new pseudo-class, `:target`, allows you to provide styles for links that were reached via clicks on an `<a>` element. You could, for instance, style a div with `display: none` (hiding it) but make it visible when the viewer clicks a "tell me more" link.

CSS3 now distinguishes pseudo-elements (fractions of actual markup elements) by prepending two colons (`::before`, `::first-letter`). It also mandates the continued acceptance of the older, single-colon form. Using `:before` (not `::before`) will continue to work in all browsers. The double-colon form will not. At present, there is no other difference between the two.

Media Queries

These have been covered in Chapter 6.

Style Attributes

The Style Attributes module is a very short document that clarifies details of the syntax of the style attribute you can use in HTML tags. If you have been using this attribute when an element in your markup needs style(s) that apply to no other element, you are using the attribute correctly.

Candidate Recommendations

Candidate Recommendations are considered "stable" and ready for vendor implementation. They may be subject to detailed corrections and clarifications, but you can use them with confidence (assuming that the "caniuse" status is satisfactory for your needs). As you know from the history of CSS 2 and 2.1, in extreme circumstances a Candidate Recommendation may revert to a Working Draft. *Caveat frontender.*

Backgrounds and Borders

CSS 3 backgrounds may be easily positioned to cover the `<body>` element to suit your design. An image may be stretched to 100% in both directions. Tiling may be specified to adjust to whole numbers of repeats (sized by the browser as needed).

Borders are substantially unchanged except that you may use images and you may use radii at the corners. We caution against the use of unneeded images (pages that are slow to load may be abandoned before your intended viewer sees your great borders). We devote Chapter 8 to the great power of the simple border radius (which costs only tens of bytes).

This specification also includes box shadows. See Go Online 7e, text shadows, for box shadow details.

The specification of this module (see the Companion Page for links) is a model of clarity.

Conditional Rules

These have been covered in Chapter 6.

Image Values and Replaced Content

The *Image Values and Replaced Content* module specifies a lot of CSS that you may want to begin using immediately. It also specifies lengths measured in screen pixels (currently as few as 72 per inch—about 30 per cm—on a desktop monitor, up to over 300 per inch on a high-end phone). We avoid these to keep our pages relatively hardware independent.

You will be able to specify image fragments, slicing as needed from a whole image file.

Importantly, you will be able to use gradients, linear and radial as a very low-cost alternative to images. (Again, gradients cost only tens of bytes. Downloading 100 bytes takes one millisecond on a very slow phone connection. Downloading an image may take a third of a second before the actual image content can start.) Gradients can be as simple as two-color washes or as complex as your color imagination likes. They may be horizontal, vertical or at any angle you like. Radial gradients may be centered or off center. We strongly urge the use of linear gradients backed up by a simple single color (for MSIE's older browsers). Radial gradients are not, as yet, widely supported, but may be available by the time you read this.

Go Online 7c illustrates linear gradients.

Online: Knowits > CSS II > Online > 7 > 7c

Marquee

The first great compromise in the browser wars, last century, was between Netscape and Microsoft. The former had added the non-standard `<blink>` tag; the latter had added `<marquee>`. The compromise was simple. Netscape dropped `<blink>` and Microsoft dropped `<marquee>`. Both tags were heartily disliked.

This specification makes the `<marquee>` tag into a standardized property. With apologies to editor Bert Bos, we are not fans.

Multi-Column Layout

Wide physical media (think newspapers) have long divided their content into columns. It is much easier to read a width comfortable to the eye. This fact is well known to those with wide monitors, too.

The ability to divide high-text content into multiple columns makes it easy to split your content into readable widths. This may be combined with media queries or a little JavaScript to make reading easy for your visitors. This technique, as Go Online 7d shows, fits neatly between fluid and responsive layout techniques.

Online: Knowits > CSS II > Online > 7 > 7d

The specification lets you adjust column widths and insert vertical dividers. If you use nothing but the `column-count` property you will get the layout your browsers' experts consider optimal. We recommend taking good advice when it's available.

That said, there is a long way to go before this is an adequate feature. Widows and orphans (sensibly defaulting to two) are still not correctly handled in all browsers. Headings (they should not be orphaned at the bottom of one column if the content they head starts another column) are provided in the specifications but not in browsers.

One hopes that some day in the near future, one's headings will become smart enough to stick to the following paragraph. (In some browsers, the widow/orphan problem has been repaired. We did nothing but retest and then smile as we saw the widows and orphans disappear at the tops and bottoms of our columns.)

Speech

This specification provides additional properties for use in aural browsers.

Values and Units

As this is written, these potentially invaluable new standards are not usable in some phones (Opera mini, Android browser, Blackberry and IE mobile) and in most IE browsers (10 and lower). Keep testing (and asking **caniuse.com**).

Among others, the new specification provides for vw and vh (width and height percentages, relative to the viewport) as well as viewport-relative minima and maxima. These will change layout work that is now very difficult into layout work that is simple.

Flexible Box Layout

According to the specification, "... In the flex layout model, the children of a flex container can be laid out in any direction, and can 'flex' their sizes, either growing to fill unused space or shrinking to avoid overflowing the parent."

This specification comes complete with new display properties, designed to provide the ultimate flexibility in two-dimensional layout. It reminds us of Sun's *GridBagLayout* for the Java language: able to solve any layout problem if you could tolerate its complexity. In Java, programmers found that combining the simpler layout models was easier than wrestling with the *GridBagLayout*.

The blogosphere has not yet been inundated with "how-to-flex-layout" posts, though this is, according to **caniuse.com**, a widely available feature.

Text Decoration

In CSS 2.1 you could specify overlines and underlines. In CSS 3 you can specify exactly where the underline should be drawn. (Just below the baseline? Below the lowest descender? To the left or right of your east Asian characters?) And you can specify lots of additional text decorations.

For those who lamented the fate of text shadows (specified in CSS 2 but dropped from CSS 2.1) you will be glad to have them back, and with interesting options, as Go Online 7e shows.

Online: Knowits > CSS II > Online > 7 > 7e

This Go Online also includes box shadows, which are specified in the same way. It does not explore the non-shadow decorations. We recommend the specification (link on Companion Page). It's well illustrated.

For those who really liked <blink>, it is also brought back as a CSS property. For those who heartily disliked <blink>, it is deprecated—you can use "animation" to make your text blink, if you must. (See `marquee`, above.)

Cascading and Inheritance

A variety of conditions not totally clear in CSS 2.1 are clarified here. Generally, this is more relevant to implementers than to authors. One important point: if you use a shorthand (e.g., `border: 1px solid green`) all shorthand properties that you don't specify default to their inherited value, if any, or to their initial value if there is no inherited value.

Fonts

Fonts Level 3 represents a vast expansion of the limited capabilities in CSS 2.1. If your field requires it (languages, archeology, typography) you must go there on your own. The specification is very clear, well-illustrated and very long. If you were content to use default font families, you can ignore this module.

Cursive fonts, more precisely specified than in CSS 2.1, are not yet correctly supported in any browser we've tested (December, 2013). Figure 7-1 shows generic fonts in one popular browser. It only gets two of the five "standard" generics correct. As always, test.

This is a generic "serif" font.

This is a generic "sans-serif" font.

This is a generic "monospace" font.

This is a generic "cursive" font.

This is a generic "fantasy" font.

Figure 7-1

Go Online 7f shows the status of default families in current browsers.

Online: Knowits > CSS II > Online > 7 > 7f

Mobile and TV Profiles

Listed here for completeness, both these Candidate Recommendations are listed as "status unknown" and may never become recommendations. Both were attempts to define subsets of CSS appropriate for devices of limited compute power. Both may have been overtaken by the rapid increase in hardware capabilities. Today's low-end phone has more compute power than a 2008 desktop (the year Mobile became a Candidate Recommendation). Either may be used by the student as a checklist of the most important CSS 2.1 properties.

Last Call

A Working Draft is promoted to Last Call when, as the name suggests, it is nearly stable, ready for implementation and approaching the point when changes (no matter how constructive) will be postponed to the next revision. If the implementers had not yet begun, this is the point at which they start to convert ideas to working code.

In theory, the W3C committees hand specifications to implementers after a consensus is achieved. In fact, implementers are active committee participants, which is very useful. Ideas that are impossible to code are rejected early. Ideas which are impractical to code are considered carefully. Ideas that seem onerous to code but are, in fact, easy to implement are added.

Basic UI

Reverted (17 Jan., 2012) from Candidate Recommendation to Last Call, Working Draft, this module is being trimmed to delete features not sufficiently widely implemented for CR status. One of the features not being trimmed is the `box-sizing` property. This line is almost magical:

```
box-sizing: border-box;
```

With that, the size of a block-level element (`width` and `height`) includes `padding` and `border`s. The caniuse summary currently (April, 2014) says this is available in all browsers except Blackberry, MSIE 8 and earlier, and Opera Mini. Firefox still requires the `-moz-` prefix.

The two boxes in Listing 7-1 are the same 300 pixels wide. The border and padding declarations for the first box are not shown, because they do not matter. It's width (measured at the outside of the borders) is 300 pixels. (Sorry to say, `box-sizing: border-box` is not universally available.)

Listing 7-1

```
#box1 {
    box-sizing: border-box;
    position:   relative;
    width:      300px;
}

#box2 {
    border:     wheat ridge 5px;
    padding:    3px;
    position:   relative;
    width:      284px;
}
```

Counter Styles

CSS 2.1 has good capability for generating counters (for use with ordered lists, document section numbers and so on). These work with most western languages. This module extends and expands those capabilities to cover all languages.

Masking

At present, (December, 2013) masking is only available in browsers built on the WebKit engine (Chrome, Opera and Safari), which is not promising if you are looking for immediately useful properties. Briefly, clipping allows you to remove portions of an image by cutting off portions horizontally or vertically. Masking allows you to draw any shape on an image (a mask) and cut off all portions that fall outside (or inside) that mask. This specification works well with SVG. SVG has not, as yet, achieved much popularity.

Text

You can safely ignore the Text Level 3 module, unless you regret the demise of justified type—once the standard for books. The additions here may make it possible to justify text without sacrificing readability, as was once done successfully by hand.

Shapes

Currently, you can use 3D transformations to manipulate rectangular 3D shapes. The cube is the most popular shape in demonstrations. The only building block available in the HTML/CSS universe is the block (rectangular unless you use border radii creatively). Rectangles severely limit the 3D capability. With a more flexible shape system, we would take a giant step forward toward 3D. It remains to be seen whether the shapes module will provide what is needed.

The Shapes module, as currently written, allows floats of irregular shapes and assists in wrapping text next to these shapes. Absent at least a transformable triangle shape, CSS 3D may be of very limited use. As currently written, the shapes module is in Last Call status and does not provide transformable shapes.

Writing Modes

The Writing Modes module accommodates worldwide writing systems by breaking down flow into an inline and a block component. Western languages flow left-to-right within a line (inline flow) and lines are stacked, top-to-bottom (block flow). By contrast Semitic languages' inline flow is right-to-left and block flow is again top to bottom. Asian languages often have top-to-bottom inline flow with left-to-right (Mongolian) or right-to-left block flow.

Those of us who work in Western languages can ignore these complications, though we appreciate the efforts of others who have worked these complications into a single, universal system.

Compositing and Blending

What happens when two images overlap? Without control of opacity, the image in front (closer to the viewer) hid the image in back. Now it's not so simple. This specification, which is clearly written and profusely illustrated, would be a good place to start to make "Porter Duff operators" a part of your working vocabulary.

Syntax

This module is important to implementers, not authors. Sample issue: suppose we were expecting a URL, but someplace in the middle we came to an invalid character. How would we "skip over" the remainder of the invalid URL to find the next CSS rule or declaration? Having all implementations answer questions like these in the same way is vital to having your pages render the same way in different browsers. Our thanks to everyone who worries about such things.

Anxiously Awaited

Animations

Currently a Working Draft and not expected to reach Last Call in the immediate future, animations let you change styles while your viewer watches your page. If you can change the position of an element in rapid, small steps you can fool the human eye into perceiving motion, of course. Animations let you add the time dimension to your 2D SVG and canvas elements. We cover animations in Chapter 10.

Transformations

If you describe an object's coordinates in space (such as specifying left, top, width and height of a div) you can specify transformations of the object. You can "translate" (move) the object by changing its left and/or top coordinates. By a bit of non-trivial mathematics you can also compute new coordinates rotating a rectangle 30 degrees clockwise around its center. Transformations provide the difficult math in a ready-to-use form that lets you specify "rotate 30 degrees clockwise, please" and, with no math to worry about, your div will be rotated. (Critically important: your div's content, such as text and graphics, rotate along with the div.) This is the subject of Chapter 9.

Transitions

A transition, in CSS, is the building block for more extended animations. You might specify that a div with `left: 100px` become a div with `left: 200px` when the mouse hovers over it. It would hop to the right on hover. It would hop back when the mouse left.

A transition lets you also specify, "make this change over 2 seconds, please" and the hop suddenly becomes a smoothly animated slide to the left or right. When you combine transitions with transformations, impossible display tricks become simple. Your page loads your heading, to which you want to attract your visitor's attention. Once the page is loaded, your heading wraps itself in a border and rotates 30 degrees, counter-clockwise. (We cover transitions in Chapter 10.) Transitions make transformations much more compelling. And they are by far the simplest way to add animations to your pages.

Project

We added media queries—based on width—to our project's stylesheet. (See the Project, Site Analysis, Chapter 6.) Our ranges are under 300 pixels, 300 through 600, and above 600. We tested by varying the size of text in `<h1>` and in `<p>` elements (fixing two of the issues in the 'All' category).

While we were styling our `<h1>` elements, we added text shadows.

A rule of thumb to follow for text shadows (or deliberately violate, but not without some thought): Less is more. Minimal offsets, fully blurred and in very light colors.

To view our site before we made it multi-device capable, visit the HTML version at:

Online: Knowits > HTML I > Project

The multi-device version:

Online: Knowits > CSS II > Project

(Almost all changes were done in the stylesheet, not the HTML.)

Quiz

1) CSS 3 is the name of
   a) the latest CSS standard.
   b) the CSS Level 3 modules, collectively.
   c) the current proposed CSS standard.
   d) the current proposed CSS Working Draft.

2) Current Level 3 Recommendations include
   a) border radii, box shadows and selectors.
   b) color, selectors and media queries.
   c) box shadows, selectors and media queries.
   d) border radii, box shadows and selectors.

3) The `:hover` selector is an example of
   a) a "user action" pseudo-class that was formerly called a "dynamic" pseudo-class.
   b) a "dynamic" pseudo-class that was formerly called a "user action" pseudo-class.
   c) a "dynamic" pseudo-element that was formerly called a "user action" pseudo-element.
   d) none of the above.

4) Candidate Recommendations
   a) are Proposed Recommendations waiting for W3C management approval.
   b) can be voted up or down, but not changed.
   c) are considered stable, ready for implementation.
   d) should not be used when creating style sheets.

5) Gradients
   a) can be used as background images.
   b) are all ready for regular use.
   c) are ready for radial, but not linear, use.
   d) are limited to two colors.

6) Multiple columns are
    a) simple and robust.
    b) simple, but not robust with respect to headings.
    c) simple and robust with respect to orphans and widows.
    d) fully supported in all MSIE versions.

7) The flexible box layout is
    a) powerful but not simple.
    b) limited in features, but very simple.
    c) rich in features and still simple.
    d) not intended for responsive designs.

8) Generic font families are
    a) your best choice if you are not an expert in typography.
    b) your best choice if you do not need a cursive font.
    c) a good choice, except for MSIE's sans-serif font.
    d) a good choice for all sans-serif and monospace fonts.

9) CSS 3's Writing Modes can accommodate
    a) Western inline and block flows.
    b) Western block flows and east Asian inline flows.
    c) any combination of inline and block flows.
    d) east Asian inline flows with right-to-left block flows.

10) Transitions are
    a) used between CSS animations.
    b) a basic part of all CSS animations.
    c) an alternative to CSS transformations.
    d) a basic part of all CSS transformations.

8 Border Radii

One of the stylistic highlights of what was called "Web 2.0" was the rectangle with rounded corners. In the old days, the frontend engineer was given a PSD (Photoshop output file) from which he used his electronic scissors to cut out the corners. These became images that were fit into the corners of divs. If done skillfully, the div looked like it had rounded corners.

Today one simply specifies:

```
border-radius: 20px;
```

The rounded corners are now so easy and so common that no one notices.

As rounded corners are a simple, decorative touch (like box and text shadows) there is no need to worry about browsers that don't support CSS 3. If the div with border radii is viewed in IE 8 it has square corners. A better browser will make it look better, but the IE 8 viewer will still see all the content.

But round corners are just the beginning of the uses of border radii. The W3C Backgrounds and Borders Module WG gave us so many possibilities that it almost makes us forget that the CSS box model limits us to rectangular shapes.

History

Prior to CSS 3, boxes had square corners. It was obvious to all that the tedious business of cutting and pasting graphic images to get round corners was a waste of expensive engineering time. The original CSS WG proposal, to provide a border-radius property, was readily accepted.

But this was one of those cases where the committee developing the specification was able to expand the idea in interesting ways.

First, why should the property apply to all four corners? Wouldn't it be interesting to permit different radii on different corners?

Then the idea of ovals was suggested. If the radius could be specified separately for length and height, an oval corner could be created. This would go significantly past the "Web 2.0" round corners.

Borders with four separately specified, elliptical corners were in the W3C WG draft as early as 2002. Vendors were implementing these ideas, with vendor-specific syntax, until the end of the last decade. We enjoy a full standard today, implemented in the current versions of all major browsers.

The companion page links to a video (the only video for this volume) of a talk by CSS WG Invited Expert Lea Verou, which she titled "The Humble Border Radius." She illustrates her talk with a simple cartoon character that proves to be well-supplied with high-tech corners.

Verou argues that the `border-radius` property would be correctly called the "corner radius" property, the radius of the outside edge of the border. The radius of the inside edge of the border is the corner radius minus the border's width. Unfortunately, only positive radius values are allowed.

Circles

The variety of shapes that can be created in CSS 3 all start with the box model plus the `border-radius` property. We begin with the original requirement: rounding the corners of otherwise square boxes.

Figure 8-1 shows "square" elements with circular border radii.

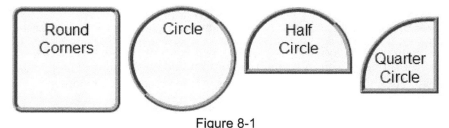

Figure 8-1

Round Corners

Every DOM element that you see on the screen is a box, courtesy of the CSS box model. Boxes with round corners have become so simple that no one notices them. You simply specify the element's `border-radius` property with a length value:

```
border-radius: 20px;
```

Go Online 8a shows a variety of basically rectangular elements with round corners.

Online: Knowits > CSS II > Online > 8 > 8a

Circles

To create a circle you simply increase the size of the round corners of a
square element until there are no straight sides between the corners.
Note: the size of a square element is the height/width plus the padding
plus the border width.

Half Circles

The first additional feature of the `border-radius` property is that you
may specify the corners individually (clockwise, from top-left). So a half
circle is done by rounding two adjacent corners. For the half circle in
Figure 8a:

```
border-radius: 60px 60px 0 0;
```

As with borders, you can also specify two or three values, but this will
save a very small bit of typing in return for coding that almost no one can
read. Stick to one value for all corners or one value for each corner.

A system for naming the corners is also part of the standard. If you
specify all four you only need to remember that they are specified
clockwise, from the top-left.

Quarter Circles

The same technique used for half circles will get a quarter circle if you
round just one corner. Again, the corners are specified clockwise, starting
from the top-left.

One of the tricky bits of using border radii is that the underlying shape is
still a rectangle. If your element encloses text, the enclosed text is
unhappily ignorant of the visible shape. It "thinks" your element is still a
rectangle. You'll have some positioning to do. (Padding is usually the
easiest way, but don't forget that increasing padding increases the
element's size.)

Full and fractional circles (pizza!) are shown in Go Online 8b.

Online: Knowits > CSS II > Online > 8 > 8b

Ovals

If one value specifies a round corner, two values (width and height) specify an oval corner. To be more exact, these values specify an elliptical corner but the ellipse's focal points are horizontal or vertical. (In Chapter 9 we rotate elements, which eliminates this constraint in most browsers.)

Figure 8-2 shows "rectangles" using oval corners.

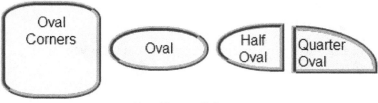

Figure 8-2

Elliptical Corners

The second additional feature added to plain border radii was the ability to specify horizontal and vertical radii separately. You separate them with a slash:

```
border-radius: width(s) / height(s);
```

Go Online 8c shows a variety of basically rectangular elements with elliptical corners.

Online: Knowits > CSS II > Online > 8 > 8c

Ellipses

As with the circle, an ellipse is simply made by increasing the border radii until there are no straight sides remaining. Warning: behavior is well-defined but still tricky if your border radii exceed the total size available. The best practice is to limit the sum of the radii on adjacent corners to the total size of the element you are styling. Exceeding the total will impact the non-adjacent corners, which can be very surprising.

Half and Quarter Ellipses

Half and quarter ellipses are made the same way as half and quarter circles: just radius the corners of two adjacent corners for a half, only one corner for a quarter.

When you specify individual corners, we recommend you specify all four separately:

```
border-radius: wid wid wid wid/hgt hgt hgt hgt;
```

Again, the specification is clockwise from top-left. You may use different numbers of values on the two sides of your "/" but you are likely to confuse yourself, not to mention anyone trying to read your code. Keep it simple.

Full and fractional ellipses are shown in Go Online 8d.

Online: Knowits > CSS II > Online > 8 > 8d

Other Shapes

See the Companion Page, "Other Shapes" for links to simple shapes, such as the ones here, and amazing shapes (triangles, hearts, yin/yang) created with amazing tricks. There is also a separate CSS Shapes Module, but that is geared toward placing text beside other shapes rather than creating shapes.

Decorated Rectangles

We use the adjective "decorated" to describe boxes that use border radii in asymmetric fashions to add visual interest. Figure 8-3 shows examples.

Figure 8-3

The two boxes on the left in Figure 8c show asymmetric corner treatments, one with a single decorated corner and the other with two corners sporting different radii. The pair on the right mates two boxes with complementary radius treatments. (See this volume's Project.)

Rectangular shapes and shape combinations with decorated corners are shown in Go Online 8e.

Online: Knowits > CSS II > Online > 8 > 8e

Eggs and Shields

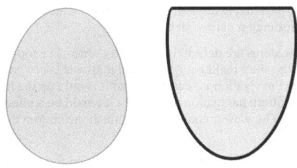

Figure 8-4

Egg-shaped and shield-shaped DOM elements are shown in Figure 8-4 and created in Go Online 8f. Also, see Verou's presentation for an adorable bouncing egg. Martin's *JavaScript Inheritance and Object Programming* book features a windowing UI based on divs in the browser. Courtesy of the border radius, it uses shield-shaped windows (among others).

As the Go Online example shows, the egg and shield shapes are surprisingly similar. (For a shield, slice the bottom off the egg. Balance the remainder on its head.)

> ### Online: Knowits > CSS II > Online > 8 > 8f

CSS is limited today to using the shapes you can create from rectangles with symmetric and asymmetric border radii. While you cannot achieve some shapes (a Valentine's Day heart cannot be done with just four corners) the possibilities are still infinite. Apply your own imagination. See also the Companion Page for links to a wide variety of other shapes, including the "impossible" heart shape.

Project

We planned two items for our project, this chapter. (See "Project," Chapter 6.) First, we wanted to fix the top-of-page navigation, an item that is important for all pages. We also wanted to address the problem of the bottom-of-page navigation on the home page, which required horizontal scrolling on narrow devices.

Note that these items are definitely in priority order. The top-of-page navigation is the site's main navigation and it affects every page. The bottom-of-page navigation is secondary and it is only on the home page. If we left the bottom navigation unchanged it would be a minor inconvenience. The viewer could scroll while at the bottom or go back to the top of the page.

While we were working on the navigation, we tried rounding the corners of the link elements. We didn't like the result. (Test on your own.) We also tried adding box shadows. We liked the result, as you can see. (Again, test on your own.)

We did manage to use border radii to provide two interesting boxes around the top navigation and the titles. By rounding the top-right corner of one and the bottom-left corner of the other we tied them together nicely without getting in the way of their functionality. Try it on your own site. Don't do it if it doesn't work.

To view our site before we made it multi-device capable, visit the HTML version at:

Online: Knowits > HTML I > Project

The multi-device version:

Online: Knowits > CSS II > Project

(Almost all changes were done in the stylesheet, not the HTML.)

Quiz

1) The Backgrounds and Borders Module working draft included today's border radius features in
  a) 2002.
  b) 2004.
  c) 2006.
  d) 2008.

2) Circles are made by
  a) images created with a package such as Photoshop.
  b) using large, circular border radii.
  c) using special 'circle' syntax.

3) Using CSS 3's `border-radius` property you can make
  a) arbitrary sections of a circle.
  b) half and quarter circles.
  c) half, quarter and eighth circles.

4) Oval (elliptical) corners are made by specifying
  a) width, then height radii, separated by a slash.
  b) two separate border radius properties.
  c) four "width/height" pairs.

5) For browsers that do not support transformations, ellipses may be specified with
  a) horizontal focal points.
  b) horizontal or vertical focal points.
  c) vertical focal points.
  d) none of the above.

6) "Decorated" rectangles use
  a) asymmetric border radii.
  b) one or two corner radii.
  c) three corner radii.
  d) all of the above.

7) Egg-shaped "rectangles" use
    a) radii symmetric about the long axis.
    b) radii symmetric about a perpendicular to the long axis.
    c) neither of the above.

8) For a vertical shield, the total of the widths of the radius specifications of the top-left and top-right corners is
    a) the width of the shield.
    b) the width plus the border-width of the shield.
    c) small, relative to the width of the shield.
    d) the width, border-width and padding of the shield.

9) For an egg shape, the radii
    a) must total the width of the egg.
    b) must total the height of the egg.
    c) must total the both width and height, including borders and padding.
    d) must be less than the width and height, including borders and padding.

10) The inside radii of a corner are equal to
    a) the specified radii minus the border width.
    b) the specified radii.
    c) one half the specified radii.
    d) the average of the width and height radii.

9 Transformations

The box model provided the underlying shape for all CSS. It provided the only shape, the rectangle, until CSS 3's Transformations module added "affine transformations" to it. (Correctly, the Transformations module is still a working draft. All major browsers, however, already provide 2D and most 3D transformations. You can use them today.)

Affine mathematics is the study of parallel lines. We will "study" it here, briefly, via a thought experiment. Begin with a large desk in front of you. Raise all the clutter 20 inches (50 cm) so you have no obstructions. Now place a sheet of graph paper on top of the desk. (Magical graph paper. Its lines are infinitely thin but quite visible. The lines are all perfectly drawn to be absolutely parallel and perpendicular.)

Our graph paper would be infinitely wide, but that is a nuisance, even in a thought experiment. Make yours a convenient size. Begin by noting that if you push the paper away from yourself, pull it toward yourself, slide it left or right, the lines are still parallel. Moving it (called a "translation") is our first example of an affine transformation. All straight lines remain straight lines. (If you don't insist on mathematical rigor, this math is fun and easy!)

Ready to go on? Try rotating your graph paper. Stick a pin in the center and then turn it. All the lines on the paper are still straight lines, of course. So this is another affine transformation, called, sensibly, "rotation."

Now let's try another. This one makes an easy thought experiment, though it's harder otherwise. Fix a metal straightedge to the bottom of your paper. Turn on the special magnet that clamps it to your desktop. Now fix another metal straightedge to the top of your paper. Last, grab the top straightedge and slide it to the right. Your paper stretches. All the vertical lines are now diagonals, pointing up and to the right. But they are all still straight lines. You have "skewed" your paper, our last affine transformation.

You'll be glad to k\now that these transformations are almost as easy in CSS as they are in thought. And you'll be amazed at how useful they are, especially in 3D.

History

Transformations allow the drawing of geometric figures (in two or three dimensions) on the flat (well, sort of flat) surface of a computer display. Lets start with a very simple case: you know that a screen rectangle is painted by lighting all the pixels within given horizontal and vertical bounds. We want to rotate this rectangle some number of degrees, clockwise. Which pixels should we turn on and off to achieve this?

Fortunately, our forebears have been working on the math, quite successfully, going back a bit more than two thousand years. We'll ask them to help us out.

Aristotle speculated that the world was round and Pythagoras (prover of the famous theorem) agreed. By about 200 BCE, Eratosthenes (Greek mathematician, working in Egypt) used angles and the circumference of the circle to actually measure the diameter of our planet. He came close (though nobody knows exactly how close, because we aren't quite sure how long his units of measure were in modern units). He might have been within a few percent.

This field, the measurement of the earth, is called "geodesy" or "geodetics." It involves a good bit of math because you can't really measure the earth's diameter with a tape measure.

An Indian astronomer/mathematician computed the earth's circumference within a percent or so, about the time of Muhammad. (The Roman Empire had recently fallen, invaded by "barbarians" from the northeast.) Three centuries later, Islamic astronomers in what is now Syria got the answer right to within a tenth of a percent. The mathematics of trigonometry and algebra was then known, and obviously correct, at least in the southwest part of Asia. (Europeans were lost in what they now call the Dark Ages.)

But the centers of learning moved north and west and by the eighteenth century, European mathematicians were extending the mathematics of geodesy, trigonometry and algebra, working on more advanced problems. Among other directions, these led, in the nineteenth century, to the development of matrix algebra and the geometry of affine transforms.

We "studied" affine transforms in our thought experiments. Matrix algebra, when added to trigonometry, proved perfect for specifying affine transforms. Multiply one set of vertices (say, the intersection of lines on a sheet of graph paper) by the correct transformation matrix and you have the set of vertices for the rotated vertices (or your rotated graph paper).

Now we fast forward to the development of the computer and then to computer graphics. Early programmers in the field recognized that matrix algebra and affine transforms provided a solid foundation for solving all the problems involved in mapping "rays" (lines, such as rays of light) from 3D geometry onto the 2D surface of a screen. Rotating a rectangle is simple once you know the matrix algebra underlying affine transforms.

More important for us, rotating a rectangle is simple once pioneering programmers have worked out the math. We just say, "rotate this div 30 degrees clockwise, please." (We will say that in CSS, of course. That becomes #this_div{ transform: rotate(30deg); }.)

Our Companion Page webliography links to the exciting developments of geodesy and traces them forward from Pythagoras up to late 20th century computer graphics texts. Importantly, it links from the early 21st century desire to simply rotate a rectangle (a div, of course) to the recognition by the W3C CSS Working Group that rotation was just one of the possible affine transforms. If you could do one, you could do them all.

We'll do 2D transforms, then move on to 3D.

2D Transformations

There are a number of 2D affine transformations, four of which (the ones we worked out in our thought experiment) are all we really need. The "translation" transformation is the one that moves a rectangle. "Rotation" allows you to break free from the strict horizontal and vertical layouts of the CSS box model. To "scale" a rectangle is to uniformly alter its size. (In terms of a div, that would be to change its width or height.) Last of our four is to "skew" (or "shear") which lets you transform a rectangle into a parallelogram.

Realize that when you "style" a div you are providing 2D coordinates. The left and top properties (or right and bottom) locate the x and y positions of one corner. The width and height properties are all you need for the other three corners.

Translations

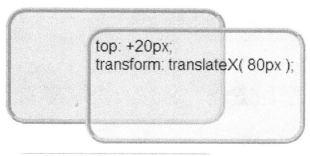

top: +20px;
transform: translateX(80px);

Figure 9-1

Figure 9-1 illustrates a translation transformation. You can move a div (or other element) simply by changing a position property, such as `left` or `top`. Why use translation?

To date (and we expect it to continue) transformations have been implemented using the GPU, graphics processing unit, of the computer (from smartphones on up). The GPU is a second computer within the computer, optimized for parallel processing (making multiple calculations simultaneously) and that means optimized for graphic transformations. The GPU contains many very simple processors that all share a portion of the graphics computations. Although much slower for general computing, it may be five to 25 times faster than the CPU for the parallel calculations needed for graphics.

Your browser is probably single-threaded (uses just one processor) in its use of the CPU (even if your CPU has more than one core). But browsers can use multi-threaded code (using all available processors) in the GPU. This means that graphics transformations, when animated, can be buttery smooth. (We'll be using these buttery smooth, 3D animations in Chapter 10. To be precise, "buttery" means running at the refresh rate of the display which is about twice as fast as the frame rate of movies.)

So we recommend that you promptly adopt transformations whenever they are available. They are only a small bit more trouble than changing a position property. To move a div 100px down, 200px right, you do this:

```
transform: translateY(100px) translateX(200px);
```

(Pay attention to the order of your transformations. The commutative property—the one that says (A + B) = (B + A)--doesn't always hold. Remember that it doesn't hold for subtraction or division, either.)

Go Online 9a shows 2D translations.

Online: Knowits > CSS II > Online > 9 > 9a

Rotations

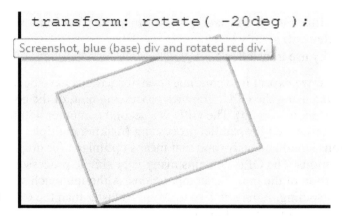

```
transform: rotate( -20deg );
```
Screenshot, blue (base) div and rotated red div.

Figure 9-2

Figure 9-2 illustrations a rotation transformation. Unlike translations, which you could do without transforms (though they might not be so smooth), rotations leave the world of CSS 2.1 behind. They free you from the horizontal- and vertical-only rules of the box model. To rotate a div (or any other element) just specify the number of degrees:

```
transform: rotate(30deg);
```

Of course, you can rotate clockwise or counter clockwise. To rotate the other way, just use a negative:

```
transform: rotate(-30deg);
```

Is a positive number of degrees clockwise or counter-clockwise? We don't know.

Actually, in the simplest case, we do know, but we try to forget. It gets too complex, too quickly. Picture a grandfather (tall case) clock. Stand facing it. Now turn it 180 degrees, so it faces away from you. Was that turn clockwise? (We didn't specify. Let's try again.) Turn it by pushing the right side away with your right hand while you pull the left side toward you with your left hand. Now, was that turn clockwise? (If you think we were specific this time, we tricked you. It depends on whether you were above the clock, facing down, or below the clock, facing up.)

Now for the simple rule for angular direction: try it! If it's wrong, stick in a minus sign (or delete the minus sign, if you had one). That rule works perfectly for even the most complex, 3D rotations.

Go Online 9b lets you try some on your own. Importantly, it shows a use for rotation that could be applied to a retail site immediately.

Online: Knowits > CSS II > Online > 9 > 9b

Now, what do you do if your div (or other element) has child elements? Here's where this gets incredibly powerful: you just rotate! The child elements all rotate, too.

The default rotation is often what you want. Your element rotates around its center. If this is not what you want you change the "origin" of the rotation. Go Online 9b also shows how this is done. It's hard to explain so the Go Online draws pictures.

Scales

Figure 9-3

Figure 9-3 illustrates a scale transformation. You make an element larger or smaller by scaling. Again, you could use the CSS 2.1 box model properties (`width` and `height`, but only if your element is "positioned"). Scaling, however, gives buttery smooth animations, not jerky size changes. Again, everything inside the scaled element expands or contracts, too.

Are scale transformations important? After all, you could just start your element at whatever size you wanted. The short answer is yes. Your browser's "new tab" page is an example of using scale to show a small image of a larger page. Chances are, the small image is not readable, but still is enough to let you recall the whole page.

Go Online 9c shows scalings on one and two axes.

Online: Knowits > CSS II > Online > 9 > 9c

Like rotating, scaling is done from the transformation origin. By default scaling is from the center, which is often what you want. And like rotating, it is simple to use another origin.

Chapter 10 will show you how to make the transition from too-small to full-size with a buttery smooth animation, called a "transition." How many properties do you think you'll need to add for this slick effect? (Hint: if you guessed higher than one, guess lower.)

Skews

Figure 9-4

Figure 9-4 illustrates a "skew" transformation. The skew (also called "shear") allows you to convert those nice, CSS 2.1 rectangles into parallelograms. You can convert a square to a diamond shape. (And once you do that, a rotate will stand your diamond on end, so it looks like a diamond.) Go Online 9d shows that skewing is done just the same as the other transformations.

Online: Knowits > CSS II > Online > 9 > 9d

3D Transformations

Preparing for 3D

You need a div within which to create your 3D objects. We start ours with a background color so we can see it. We'll usually erase the background before we're done. While developing, we choose a background that will not conflict with the objects we will create. It gets typical div styles (size, position and so on) plus two 3D-related properties:

- `perspective`
- `perspective-origin`

The `perspective` property gets a length value. To start, make it about three times as long as the depth of the object(s) you will create. Experiment, after your objects are ready, to see what looks best.

The `perspective-origin` gets two values (space-separated): X and Y. These locate the "eye" of the viewer. The default is `50% 50%`, which you almost never want. (View a cube from its center and you will see nothing but the face closest to your eye.) A good default is `0% 0%` (top, left) which will let you see a cube's face, top and left side.

Optionally, you create one or more elements within your perspective div as parents of the objects you will treat as units. When we build a sign we will want to rotate the whole sign to an angle that we like, so we build all its components in a "sign" div. Then we only need to rotate the parent div to keep all its parts together.

For an object parent, the `transform-style` property must be provided and its value must be `preserve-3d.` This will ensure that when the parent is transformed, (skewed, rotated, translated, ...) the children all move as parts of the parent.

We also like to draw an outline, showing the size of our object(s) on the perspective div. Go Online 9e lets you try this preparation along with your first Z-axis translations.

Note: you could have multiple 3D divs with multiple viewpoints. The result is almost certain to be confusing. (If you want to be the next Salvador Dali, this might be an interesting place to start.)

Translate

In Go Online 9e you create a perspective div and three more outline-only divs. These vary their places along the Z axis: farthest, middle distance and closest. You see clearly that the closest is much larger (takes more screen real estate) although its nominal size is the same as the others. This, of course, is the essence of drawing in perspective.

Online: Knowits > CSS II > Online > 9 > 9e

Rotate

The rotation we used in 2D was, in fact, one of the three rotations possible in 3D: `rotateZ()`. In these, the final letter (X, Y or Z) denotes the axis around which we will rotate. To demonstrate this to yourself (anyone working in 3D makes these funny gestures!) go back to Go Online 9b and point your finger into your monitor. Your finger is the Z axis. You see that your 2D objects rotate around your finger.

For `rotateX()` and `rotateY()`, visualize a sheet of glass. Write a word ("flower" will work) at the top of the sheet and draw something (a flower would be appropriate) below the text.

`rotateX()`: Hold the sheet by the center of the two sides; hold it in front of you as if it were a tablet computer. Admire your work. Now let the top turn toward you. You are holding the sides, rotating along the X axis. At 180 degrees, your word is upside down at the bottom, your drawing is upside down, above the word.

`rotateY()`: Carousels, like the one you can build in Appendix A, are a good example of an object that rotates around its Y axis. To see for now, hold your sheet of glass by the top and bottom; center your fingers between the sides. Spin it around. At 180 degrees your word and drawing are both backwards. (When you build your cube you will see that it is very easy to get your text backwards.)

Go Online 9f illustrates all three rotations and the `backface-visibility` property.

Online: Knowits > CSS II > Online > 9 > 9f

Origin and rotation: the transform origin is an (X, Y) point, often specified with % values: `transform-origin: 50% 100%;`. Axes of rotation are lines, not points. The `rotateY()` around (50%, 100%) is rotation around the line Y = 100%. The X value is ignored.

Scale and Multiple Axes

Rotations rotate an object's axes along with the object. Rotations applied to child objects do not rotate the axes of the parent object. Our 3D objects can each have their own X, Y and Z axes. We'll explore this very important fact in Go Online 9g. Otherwise, scaling in 3D is a very simple extension of scaling in 2D.

Scaling in 3D adds the `scaleZ()` property to the `scaleX()` and `scaleY()` properties you've already used. Go Online 9g illustrates all of them and shows how composite objects can have multiple sets of axes.

Online: Knowits > CSS II > Online > 9 > 9g

Building a Sign

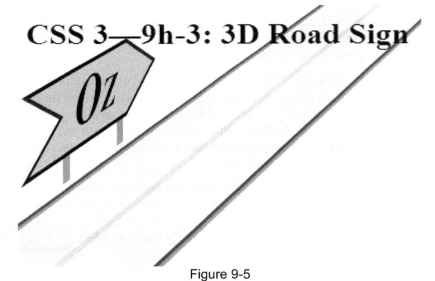

Figure 9-5

In Go Online 9h you'll build a billboard-sized sign, illustrated in Figure 9-5, that points the way alongside a road (and lets you add content over the otherwise decorative road). It's a dramatic example of adding visual "pop" with 3D perspective and rotation. 2D skews create a useful arrow element before we get to rotation.

Some notes, before you begin. We start with the big question.

Why? A designer skilled with Adobe Illustrator can easily create a graphic. If you use CSS3 3D drawing however, a new world opens up. Suppose you want the road to run more nearly across the page, but then turn out of the way of your other content. Yes, you can rotate the scene, road and sign together, with very little effort. (Animations come in Chapter 10.) JavaScript (starts in Volume III) adds another universe of possibilities.

The skeleton. We begin by using our template to create a skeletal file. Nothing special here. Use View Source in your browser if you need to clarify any details. The skeleton starts in Go Online 9h-0.

The sign. We make an arrow by skewing a div a little more than 45 degrees, and then putting it on top of another div with the opposite skew. A third div holds the sign's text in front of the first two. The sign is in Go Online 9h-1.

The road. We build the road under the sign. Some paving with a border. A second div gives us a center stripe. Rotate it 90 degrees on the X axis (origin at the top, bottom rotates toward us). Go Online 9h-2 shows the road added, but not rotated.

Final position. We finish with legs for the billboard (which help position it) and then final placement. A div for each leg would work, but there's an easier way. We use a single div with a left and right border. Sign and road are built inside a "scene" div. We rotate the scene on its Y axis. This turns sign and road together. Go Online 9h-3 shows the result.

Go Online 9h includes a menu of these sub-pages that show our steps.

Online: Knowits > CSS II > Online > 9 > 9h

Building a Cube

Figure 9-6

The classic 3D CSS demo is the rotating cube. You'll build a static cube, illustrated in Figure 9-6, in Go Online 9i, You will rotate it in Chapter 10. The "box" shape (rectangular parallelepiped, if you are mathematically inclined) is fundamental to much 3D work. You could call it the basic "building block."

One note before you go there. The specs, as written today, have a serious flaw. Positions on the Z axis cannot be specified in percents. This means that fluid 3D cannot scale nicely from phones through desktops (and on to wall-size TV monitors). Unless, of course, you find a way to get around the problem, such as the one we show in Appendix A when we build a carousel. For now we'll use the common approach in Go Online 9i, which is easier to explain (although it's more work).

Online: Knowits > CSS II > Online > 9 > 9i

Project

Transformations are so compelling that we are pretty sure you want to try them in your project website. Slow down! Don't transform anything until you can answer this question in the affirmative: Does this transform help me communicate more clearly? Transforms are easy. Useful transforms require lots of thought! (After you've got your thoughts in order, transforms are still easy.) We recommend putting this on the back burner until you've learned how to animate your transformations, next chapter.

While you're thinking about transforms as means of communication, not just as eye candy, we will return to our existing work schedule.

We planned two improvements to our site for this chapter. (See Chapter 6, "Project.") First, we wanted multi-column text for wide pages. This is an important factor where there is a lot of text (as in our "Newton said" page, where we are pretending that the *lorem ipsum* is real text). Second, and lower in priority, we wanted to make the five-abreast portraits (home and credits pages) a responsive, as-many-as-fit element.

We hope that this chapter has whet your appetite for CSS 3 transformations. We also hope that you don't use them too liberally. We resisted the temptation to add them to our project site. Try some on your own site. Be ruthless about deleting them if they are merely cute or fun (unless, of course, cute or fun are appropriate for your site—we like cute, fun sites, too).

To view our site before we made it multi-device capable, visit the HTML version at:

Online: Knowits > HTML I > Project

The multi-device version:

Online: Knowits > CSS II > Project

(Almost all changes were done in the stylesheet, not the HTML.)

Quiz

1) An affine transformation is one in which
   a) the area of the transformed shape is unchanged.
   b) the length of the perimeter of the transformed shape is unchanged.
   c) neither the area nor the perimeter of the transformed shape is changed.
   d) all straight lines in the transformed shape remain straight lines.

2) A 2D rotation transformation is a rotation around the
   a) Z axis.
   b) X axis.
   c) Y axis.
   d) none of the above.

3) A 2D translation transformation
   a) moves an element's top and/or left position.
   b) changes an element's language.
   c) repositions an element on the Z axis.
   d) none of the above.

4) A 2D scale transformation
   a) is not an affine transformation.
   b) changes the "weight" assigned to an element.
   c) requires an assigned Z-index value.
   d) changes an element's width or height.

5) A skew transformation can
   a) be applied along the Z axis.
   b) not be used with 3D elements.
   c) is not an affine transformation.
   d) change a rectangle to a parallelogram.

6) 2D rotation transformations can rotate around
   a) the X axis only.
   b) the Y axis only.
   c) the X and Y axes.
   d) the Z axis only.

7) After a 3D rotation around the Y axis,
    a) the Y axis is rotated.
    b) the X axis is also rotated.
    c) the X and Z axes are also rotated.
    d) rotations do not change the axes.

8) If a 2D skew transformation has been applied a 3D rotation will
    a) rotate the skewed element.
    b) not rotate the skewed element.
    c) will rotate the skewed element, but will undo the skew transformation.

9) The current W3C transformation specifications
    a) do not allow percentage lengths.
    b) require percentage lengths, not pixel lengths.
    c) permit all valid CSS lengths.
    d) do not allow percentage lengths for Z-axis translations.

10) To read correctly, a cube with text on all sides
    a) requires 180-degree rotations of some sides.
    b) may be built without 180-degree rotations.
    c) requires 180-degree rotation of sides that are viewed from inside.
    d) requires 180-degree rotation of sides that are viewed from outside.

10 CSSimation

"Animation," literally "giving life" refers to various means of showing motion. For us it has two meanings: CSS3 "transitions" and CSS3 "animations," the latter more precisely known as key-frame animations.

A CSS3 transition may be specified by providing two different values, applicable under different conditions, for a numeric property, such as `left`. If you specify `left: 100px;` normally, but, with the `:hover` selector suffix, you specify `left: 200px;` your element will hop from 100 to 200 when the mouse hovers over it. It will hop back when the mouse stops hovering. This hopping will be a form of motion, but it won't feel like animation.

If you specify a transition (say, "spend two seconds on any change in `left`") your element will slide when the mouse hovers, which brings it to life. (The word "animation" comes from the Latin "*animatio*," or possibly "*animare*," meaning "to give life.") It gives the illusion of life by changing position in small increments in rapid succession. (Say, moving left one pixel at a time, 60 times per second.)

Like transitions, key-frame animations specify changes that take place over time. Unlike transitions, which have only two states, an animation specifies multiple states as "key" frames and specifies the value at each state. You could specify motion in one direction, followed by motion in another direction. Again, your element will "come alive" as the changes are divided into small increments and applied very rapidly.

In fact, this animation has a very long history.

History

Cave paintings from the paleolithic era show animals changing position in a series of drawings, which suggest motion. About 4,000 years ago, Egyptians used series of drawings to suggest motion in tomb decorations.

Animation in the modern sense is about 2,000 years old. A zoetrope, one Chinese example dates to 180 CE, rotates a series of drawings behind a cylinder with slits allowing the viewer to see one drawing at a time.

Modern animation started in film in the 1890s, led by work in Edison's labs in the U.S. and the Lumiere brothers factory in France. Edison's engineers built a "kinetoscope," a single-viewer device based on a strip of film holding multiple pictures, taken over time to capture motion. The Lumiere brothers were also capturing motion on film and they were projecting their photo strips for audience viewing, very much like modern movies. Both teams created special cameras for taking the multiple shots needed to create the film.

Within a generation, these novelties became today's movies supporting a substantial industry (initially centered in Hollywood, California where the sunlight was suitable for filming on most days of the year). The term "animation" was returned to short subjects, cartoons, made by artists, not by photographing actors.

Walt Disney created the full-length film animation genre with 1937's daring *Snow White*. The film cost $1.5 million dollars, a staggering sum to spend on an untried genre in a country still suffering from the Great Depression. Would people pay to see a full-length movie, that was, in fact, just a cartoon? Disney was right; people would pay. *Snow White* was the highest grossing film of all time at its initial release and has since earned over $400 million.

Animated films have progressed. The computer is a natural tool for the repetitive drawing of frames which are only slightly different from each other. Today, Pixar Studios (now owned by Disney) has pioneered, eventually doing 100% of the art work on computer.

Beginning with the video game *Pong*, 1972, animated computer games have progressed, too, from coin-operated amusements in arcades and bars to today's home game consoles. These generate animated, 3D games on tiny computers containing more computation power than late twentieth-century supercomputers.

The power to do animations is available in today's desktop computers, tablets and smartphones. The ability to animate web pages is coming to the frontend engineer as this is written. We'll start with transitions. Their simplicity may amaze you.

Timing Functions

Before we dive into transitions, timing functions are applied to CSS animations: transitions and key-frame animations. You specify a start and finish property value and duration (in seconds or milliseconds). If you like, you also specify a timing function controlling exactly how the property changes. The simplest value is `ease` (the default).

We like the `ease` transition. It starts near full speed, runs at full speed until near the end when it slows to a graceful stop. If you like to control things you can pick one of these additional "easing" transitions:

- `ease-in` slow start, then full speed
- `ease-in-out` slow start and slow finish
- `ease-out` full speed, then slow finish

If you really like to control things, and you like math, you can specify `cubic-bezier` to shape your own curve to control the transition. If the whole idea bothers you, you can specify `linear` for a constant-speed transition. (For infinitely looping animations, `linear` is usually the best choice.) Use the Companion Page webliography to research the alternatives such as step timings.

If your transitions are quick (in Windows, minimize or restore a window —to or from the Taskbar—to view a quick transition) you probably will not see any difference between the timing functions. One study suggested that most viewers can tolerate a 0.5 second transition without getting annoyed. We suggest erring on the side of quicker transitions if you are keeping your viewer waiting. (We don't mind the quarter second or so Windows takes to shrink a window down to a position on the Taskbar. The animation shows us that it is minimizing, not closing. It's information, not just eye candy.)

Transitions

When you specify a transition, any change in property value will be applied over the duration of the transition. (No transition? The duration is zero. Instant change.)

CSS can change a property value when user action invokes a pseudo-element, The selector `xxx:hover` specifies properties when the mouse is over an element. Transitions on any of the `:hover` properties will make the changes graceful (both when hovering starts, and when it ends). Changes triggered in JavaScript (say, after the user selects an option) will also transition as specified in your CSS.

The two lines in Listing 10-1 will change a light brown background to white on hover:

Listing 10-1

```
xxx { background: wheat; }
xxx:hover { background: white; }
```

Adding `transition: background 0.5s;` is all you need to make
the color change a smooth color transition. (You'll need to be careful
about those fractional seconds, however. Is half a second fast enough to
tell your visitor that the mouse is over a clickable button? Is the button so
obviously clickable that perhaps a slower, 'just a reminder' transition is
better?)

Most properties that take a numeric value will transition smoothly. That
includes positions, sizes and colors. Some properties (`font-family`,
for instance) are non-numeric and cannot transition. Some properties
(`font-size`, for instance) are numeric but limited to a few values, so
they can transition, but they won't transition smoothly.

Opacity, either the `opacity` property or the alpha channel in an
`rgba()` (or `hsla()`) color, can let you transition between vastly
different things, such as two images. (Fade one in at the same time you
fade another out. Yes, this will make very slick buttons!)

Transitions and transformations go together like chocolate and vanilla (in
browsers that support transformations, of course).

Go Online 10a shows some examples.

Online: Knowits > CSS II > Online > 10 > 10a

A note on font sizes. If you really want text to transition smoothly try
using a 2D scaling transformation on the element containing the text. A
ten-point font scaled up by ten percent will not be as readable as an
actual eleven-point font viewed head on. But if you are rotating and/or
skewing the text container (revisit Go Online 9h-3) it will be a good
substitute.

Animations

There's a little bit of Dr. Frankenstein in all of us. It comes out, without endangering the local villagers, when we bring things to life. Animations are fun!

An animation is a set of frames shown in rapid succession. Typically, your browser will attempt to show one frame per refresh cycle. (Common rate for monitors: 60 frames per second. Most movies on film: 24fps. Old, a bit jerky, silent films: 16fps.) 60 fps exceeds the eye's ability to 'refresh' the nerves that give us vision. We perceive it as smooth motion. (Movies also look smooth, but that is because of the slight blurring in each frame. 24fps is not so smooth without the blur.)

Of course, creating 60 frames for each second of animation is a massive job, even if you are just specifying one or two properties, so CSS introduced `keyframes`. You specify a few frames' values (as few as the first and the last), and leave the browser to work out all the other frames.

In film, the main artists painted key frames and the others were drawn by the junior people. The juniors' job was called "tweening"—from "in between." You'll be happy to have your browser do the tweening.

To do CSS animations, you create a set of `keyframes` (at least the first and last). You give the set of `keyframes` a name and then use this name to specify an animation property. The animation property specifies the duration. The browser uses the duration to generate the individual frames. (You might get 120 frames for two seconds of 60 fps animation.)

`@keyframes` Rule Sets

A set of `keyframes` provides values for the first frame, called `from`, the last frame, called `to`, and zero or more intermediate frames, named with percentages. The frame named `50%` is the one half way between `from` and `to`. The `from` frame may also be called `0%` and the `to` frame may be called `100%`, so all you need to remember is that the frames are named with percentages (and you can forget `from` and `to` until you see them in other style sheets).

Assume you want a `dropdown` animation to lower an element from the top of its container down to the lower half of the container. Listing 10-2 shows the `@keyframes` rule set:

Listing 10-2

```
@keyframes dropdown {
      0% { top: 0;    } /* the "from" frame */
    100% { top: 50%; } /* the "to"   frame */
}
```

Unfortunately, you still need prefixes. At this time we are using:

* `@-webkit-keyframes name {...}`
* `@keyframes name {...}`

Note: there are unsettled issues when you use pre-Recommendation features. The WebKit (Chrome, Opera, Safari) animation starts at `0%` (or `from`) at the beginning of the delay before the animation. Firefox starts, more sensibly we think, after the delay. The cross-browser technique is to incorporate the delay into the `keyframes`: instead of a ten-second delay followed by a ten-second animation, use a twenty-second animation with identical values at `0%` and `50%`.

You can have as many CSS declarations in each keyframe rule as you like. You can declare some properties in some frames, and omit them in other frames.

`animation` **Property**

Once you have created your `keyframes` ruleset you invoke it by attaching it to an element with the `animation` property, as Listing 10-3 shows.

Listing 10-3

```
#xxx {
    animation: dropdown 5s;
}
```

The above attaches the `keyframes` ruleset named `dropdown` to the selected element (or elements—any CSS selector you like) and runs it over five seconds. There are a substantial number of additional options for the `animation` property that are covered in the examples. You can run an animation repeatedly, or infinitely, you can reverse it and so on. You can also apply all the timing functions that we met when we looked at transitions.

You will quickly find that you want user-controlled animation which CSS can only do in very simple cases, such as with `:hover` pseudo elements. For full control you'll want JavaScript, which we start in the next volume in this series.

Time to try animation. Go Online 10b shows a simple animation, moving a headline left and back.

Online: Knowits > CSS II > Online > 10 > 10b

Go Online 10c shows an animated transform, rotating a headline (it takes a bow).

Online: Knowits > CSS II > Online > 10 > 10c

Animating Your Cube

In Chapter 9 you built a cube, which you could look at from different viewpoints by changing `perspective` and `perspective-origin` properties. Now we have the tools to really bring that cube to life. We can sit right in front of it (or view it on our smartphones, held out in front of us) and watch it move and rotate, even swell and shrink, as if it were alive.

Online: Knowits > CSS II > Online > 10 > 10d

Project

When we planned our multi-device site improvements (see "Project," Chapter 6) we loaded the "nice to have, but not really necessary" improvements into our schedule for this chapter. (That is a time-tested management technique. The trick is to not make it too obvious.) We wanted to make the timeline and map responsive elements on the first page (side-by-side, space permitting, over-and-under otherwise). And we wanted the timeline and map to both permit narrower layouts on their own pages.

As luck would have it, being prepared paid off. None of our other improvements had spilled over into the time given for this chapter. Fortunately, we found a very easy solution for the home page and for making the other pages more fluid. "View Source" to see how we did it.

That left us enough extra time to add a totally unnecessary transition effect on the top-of-page navigation elements. Hover over them to see it in action. (And judge for yourself whether this is a nice little effect that only CSS 3 connoisseurs will notice, or an annoyance that we should have left out.)

To view our site before we made it multi-device capable, visit the HTML version at:

Online: Knowits > HTML I > Project

The multi-device version:

Online: Knowits > CSS II > Project

(Almost all changes were done in the stylesheet, not the HTML Fitting the map on the map page is one notable—and very simple—exception.)

All pages on our project site are now at least acceptable (most are good) between about 300 and 2000 pixels wide. There are some exceptions. The timeline needs horizontal scrolling below about 500 pixels. (Our tablet viewers have to turn their devices to landscape mode, a minor issue.)

We consider this professional quality work for an information site in early 2014. Will we be happy when we test our site on our first Samsung wristwatch? Probably not (but it would be silly to visit this site on a wristwatch). What about those new eyeglass viewers? We'll see. This technology does not stand still!

Quiz

1) The earliest known device to create animation from a sequence of illustrations was created by
    a) Edison's engineers at the end of the nineteenth century.
    b) the Lumiere brothers at the end of the nineteenth century.
    c) Persian astronomers 1200 years ago.
    d) a Chinese inventor, 2000 years ago.

2) Walt Disney's movie *Snow White* was
    a) the first full-length animated film.
    b) the highest grossing film ever when first released.
    c) both of the above.

3) Adding a `transition` between CSS property values requires
    a) just 4 CSS declarations.
    b) just 3 CSS declarations.
    c) just 2 CSS declarations.
    d) just 1 CSS declaration.

4) In setting 3D `perspective` and `perspective-origin`,
    a) negative values may be used for either.
    b) negative values may only be used for `perspective`.
    c) negative values may only be used for `perspective-origin`.
    d) negative values may not be used.

5) The default `ease` timing
    a) is a good choice for `transitions` and non-`infinite` `animations`.
    b) is a good choice for `infinite animations`.
    c) should not be used for `transitions`.
    d) starts more slowly than an `ease-in-out` timing.

6) The `from` and `to` key frames
    a) are synonyms for `0%` and `100%`.
    b) are required for all `keyframes` sets.
    c) end and start, respectively, `transitions`.
    d) end and start, respectively, `animations`.

7) Transitions apply
    a) with each click or finger touch.
    b) with each mouse hover.
    c) with each mouse hover or finger touch.
    d) with each change in a property value.

8) After an `animation`, properties
    a) remain in their `100%` keyframe value.
    b) return to their pre-animation values.
    c) switch to their `0%` keyframe value.
    d) transition to their `0%` keyframe value.

9) Z axis values
    a) may be set to percentage values.
    b) may be set indirectly by `rotateX()` or `rotateY()` transformations.
    c) may not be set by `translateZ()` transformations.
    d) may be set indirectly by skew transformations.

10) Our carousel would be improved by
    a) JavaScript-based user controls.
    b) use of `hsla()` background colors.
    c) adding images.

A – Building a Carousel

Do you like challenges? Conquer this one and even veteran frontend engineers will be impressed. Here we'll use what you've learned to create a fully fluid image carousel. If you like, your images can be less than opaque so you can see the ones in back right through the ones in front. Take a peak at Go Online A1 to see what it looks like.

Online: Knowits > CSS II > Online > A1

A cube is an extruded square with a top and bottom added. We can also extrude all the other regular polygons: pentagons, hexagons and so on. (How many sides? How's your patience? As many as you like.)

There is a bit of tricky folding required to make fully fluid extruded polygons. The W3C specification omits percentage lengths in the `translateZ()` transformation. You want your 3D objects to scale nicely in all three dimensions to fit as many devices as possible.

After you get your polygon shape, you'll add images to each side and set the object spinning on its Y axis (conveniently located in its center) The result is a treat!

Make your carousel a nice one. An animated carousel is a good example to show to potential employers or clients. The CSS is advanced and the commercial possibilities are endless. Go Online A1 shows you how.

Online: Knowits > CSS II > Online > A1

A – Building a Carousel

B – Basic Trigonometry

You probably studied the basics of sines, cosines and tangents when you were in high school. Most of us have had no occasion since to apply this knowledge. Your authors find that it crops up from time to time, but so infrequently that it requires looking up when it appears.

Suppose you want the user to select a time (to schedule an appointment) by clicking on a clock face. This makes a very quick, easy-to-use input widget but under the surface, some trigonometry is needed to translate the X, Y location of a mouse click into the time (angle of the clock hands).

And then there is the image carousel. We tried first with a spreadsheet replete with sines and cosines to compute X, Z coordinates (before we discovered that "folding" divs was easier and solved the essential problem of keeping the result fluid).

This is the quick review that we would need before grabbing our calculators.

Fundamental Ratios

Based on a right triangle, the three most common functions in trigonometry are the ratios of pairs of sides. The hypotenuse of the right triangle, the long side, is the denominator for sines and cosines. The sides at 90 degrees to each other are called "adjacent" (one side of the angle) and "opposite" (away from the angle). Figure B-1 shows these.

Figure B-1

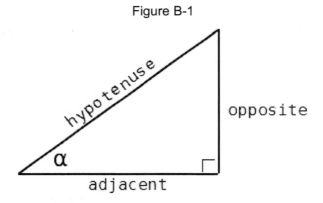

```
sine = opposite / hypotenuse

cosine = adjacent / hypotenuse

tangent = opposite / adjacent
```

Unit Circles

It is often true that embedding your right triangle in a "unit circle" (a circle that has a radius of one) saves you from a great deal of arithmetic. Figure B-2 shows regular polygons embedded in unit circles.

Figure B-2

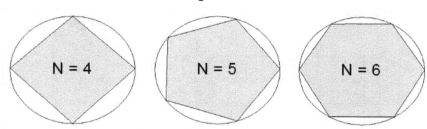

The sines and cosines of your angle are also the lengths of the adjacent and opposite sides, as shown in Figure B-3.

Figure B-3

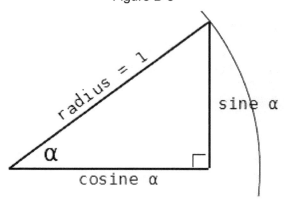

Table Headings

In laying out tables with HTML (any version of HTML prior to CSS3 transformations) we were limited to writing horizontal text above the columns. If the data in the columns did not need many pixels, we still had to have a column that was wide enough to hold the heading.

A simple solution to fitting more columns (or taking less space) is to rotate the column headings, as shown in Figure B-4.

Figure B-4

A Sample Table

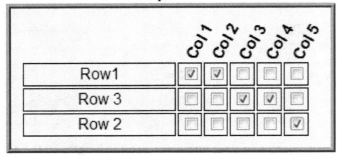

The headings in Figure B-4 are rotated 60 degrees. More than this becomes very difficult to read. (Vertical text is extremely difficult to read. Test this the first time you rotate table headings.) How wide a column is needed? That depends on the height of the heading line and the angle of rotation. For this, we need some trigonometry.

If "L" is the line-height of the heading text, and "W" is the width of the column needed for the line-height, we can calculate the relationship between L and W as shown in Figure B-5.

Figure B-5

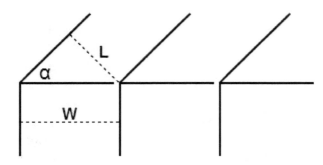

In Figure B-5, the hypotenuse of the triangle enclosing angle *alpha* is W long. The sine of *alpha,* the opposite divided by the hypotenuse, is L / W so we get:

```
sine α = L / W

L = W * sine α
```

or

```
W = L / sine α
```

You choose the more restrictive of the label line height or the column width and then use one of the above equations to find the unknown.

C – Regular Polygons

We are ready to apply our small subset of trigonometry to the problem of "drawing" regular polygons. For our carousel, we showed how you could apply CSS3 transforms to create a fluid 3D carousel with absolutely no math.

Online: Knowits > CSS II > Online > A1

However, as you go on to other forms, you will not always stumble on solutions that depend solely on "folding" your "paper" to achieve the result you seek.

We start by looking at regular polygons drawn in a unit circle. This leads quickly to a generalized method of deriving the X, Y coordinates of the vertexes (angles) in the polygons, and the ratio of the side length to the circle's radii.

Polygon in Unit Circle

By now you have become accustomed to the CSS coordinate system: 0, 0 is at the top, left corner and values increase downward and to the right. We ask you now to return to the Cartesian coordinates you used in high school math: 0, 0 is in the center; X increases to the right and Y increases going up. (The CSS, and HTML, system will be used for most of your work, but if you advance to WebGL, making heavy use of modern 3D, you will put the Cartesian coordinates back into service. 0, 0, 0 will be the center of your cyber worlds.)

To draw a regular polygon, start with a circle. Lay out a radius line. Place this base radius at 3:00 o'clock to make many future steps easier. (That's the line from 0, 0 to 1, 0 if you have a unit circle in the center.)

Then you draw additional radii around the circle at equal angles (the angle is named *alpha* in the figures). The angle, for an N-sided polygon is 360 / N. Figure C-1 shows a pentagon, N = 5, radii 72 degrees apart.

Figure C-1

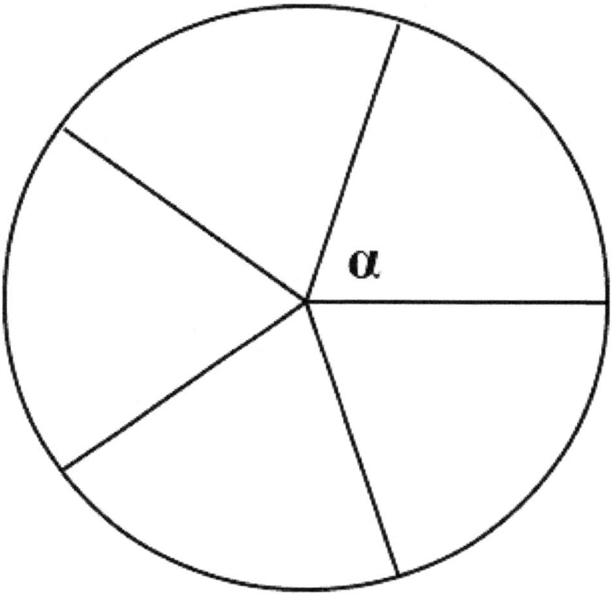

With circle and spokes you complete the polygon by connecting the intersections of the spokes and the circle. Figure C-2 shows the result and names the angle between the radii and the side *beta*.

Note that there are 180 degrees in the sum of the degrees in each angle in a triangle. In our drawing:

```
α + β + β = 180
```

Alternatively,

```
β = (180 - α) / 2
```

Figure C-2

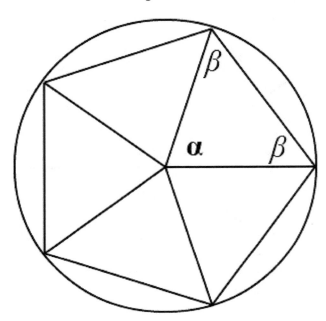

Remember that our unit circle radii are all one unit long. If we want a radius of 150 pixels, we simply declare a unit to be 150 pixels. In this example, we got a circle by starting with `height` and `width` of 300 pixels and then `border-radius` of 150 pixels.

Continuing with CSS, our radii are `divs` with a two-pixel border, top only. They are 150 pixels wide, 0 high. We created them all where the 3:00 o'clock radius remains. The second one was rotated `-72` degrees. The third one was rotated `-144` degrees (2 * -72) and so on.

For sides, we attached another div as the child of each radius and rotated it as Go Online A-1 showed.

Vertex Coordinates

Now we are ready to get the coordinates we need to draw a regular polygon using CSS. ("Vertex" is the name for a point in the mathematics of computer graphics.) We begin by drawing a line from the second corner (the intersection of the second radius with the circle) straight down to the first radius, as Figure C-3 shows.

Figure C-3

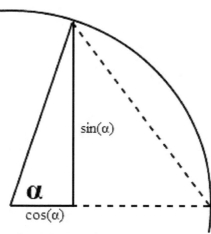

$\sin(\alpha)$

α

$\cos(\alpha)$

From there, the length of the inscribed triangle's side adjacent to *alpha* is the cosine of *alpha*. That is the value of X, in units. (Multiply by 150 for units 150 pixels long.) Similarly, the value of Y is the length of the opposite side of the inscribed triangle, which is the sine of *alpha*.

Now, a little spreadsheet (Figure C-4) lets us create all the answers we need. (Our spreadsheet works for a dozen-sided polygon. For a pentagon, we get the same coordinates for radius five that we got for radius zero, which is harmless.) Just plug in the number of sides, the length of a unit and you're done.

Figure C-4

	A	B	C	D	E
1					
2	Number of sides:		8		
3	Length of radius:		200		
4					
5		Alpha	45		
6		**Angle**	**Rads**	**X**	**Y**
7	0	0	0.000	200.0	0.0
8	1	45	0.785	141.4	141.4
9	2	90	1.571	0.0	200.0
10	3	135	2.356	-141.4	141.4
11	4	180	3.142	-200.0	0.0
12	5	225	3.927	-141.4	-141.4
13	6	270	4.712	0.0	-200.0
14	7	315	5.498	141.4	-141.4
15	8	360	6.283	200.0	0.0
16	9	405	7.069	141.4	141.4
17	10	450	7.854	0.0	200.0
18	11	495	8.639	-141.4	141.4
19	12	540	9.425	-200.0	0.0
20					

We've shown the results for an 8-sided polygon, 200 pixel radius. This is an easy one to test because you can check it without a calculator. At zero degrees (3:00 o'clock, radius zero) the vertex is (200, 0). At 45 degrees, the vertex is (141.4, 141.4). (You recognized the square root of two, we hope.)

Now there is only one problem left to solve: how long is a side of the polygon for a given radius?

Length of a Side

Figure C-5 shows another radius, bisecting angle *alpha*. Like the last inscribed triangle, the hypotenuse of this inscribed triangle is again one radius long. So again we can read the lengths directly from the diagram.

Figure C-5

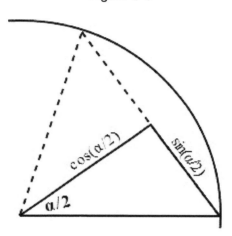

As the length of a half side is the sine of half *alpha,*

```
side length = 2 * sin(α/2)
```

(That is the length in units. Multiply by the length of the unit for the length in pixels.)

For a pentagon:

N = 5

α = 360 / N = 72

sine (α / 2) = sine (36) ~= 0.5878

side length = 0.5878 * 2 = 1.1756

Quiz Answers

I	1c,	2a,	3d,	4b,	5c,	6a,	7c,	8c,	9d,	10c
II	1c,	2a,	3c,	4d,	5c,	6b,	7b,	8c,	9b,	10a
III	1c,	2c,	3c,	4a,	5d,	6d,	7b,	8b,	9b,	10d
IV	1b,	2d,	3c,	4d,	5b,	6c,	7d,	8b,	9a,	10d
V	1c,	2c,	3c,	4b,	5d,	6c,	7d,	8a,	9b,	10c
VI	1a,	2d,	3c,	4b,	5a,	6a,	7a,	8d,	9d,	10d
VII	1b,	2b,	3a,	4c,	5a,	6b,	7a,	8d,	9c,	10b
VIII	1a,	2b,	3b,	4a,	5b,	6d,	7a,	8c,	9c,	10a
IX	1d,	2a,	3a,	4d,	5d,	6d,	7c,	8a,	9d,	10b
X	1d,	2c,	3d,	4c,	5a,	6a,	7d,	8b,	9b,	10a

www.ingramcontent.com/pod-product-compliance
Lightning Source LLC
Chambersburg PA
CBHW071156050326
40689CB00011B/2140